CULTURE SMART!

GUATEMALA

THE ESSENTIAL GUIDE TO
CUSTOMS & CULTURE

RUSSELL MADDICKS

T0300660

KUPERARD

"The real voyage of discovery consists not in seeking new landscapes, but in having new eyes."

Adapted from Marcel Proust, *Remembrance of Things Past*

ISBN 978 1 78702 363 5

British Library Cataloguing in Publication Data
A CIP catalogue entry for this book is available
from the British Library

First published in Great Britain
by Kuperard, an imprint of Bravo Ltd
59 Hutton Grove, London N12 8DS
Tel: +44 (0) 20 8446 2440
www.culturesmart.co.uk
Inquiries: publicity@kuperard.co.uk

Design Bobby Birchall

The Culture Smart! series is continuing to expand.
All Culture Smart! guides are available as e-books, and many
as audio books. For further information and latest titles visit
www.culturesmart.co.uk

RUSSELL MADDICKS is an award-winning journalist, translator, and travel writer. A graduate in Economic and Social History from the University of Hull, England, he has spent the last twenty years traveling, living, and working in Latin America and for ten years covered news in the region for the BBC.

He has visited Central America on many extended trips, always finding some new and unusual facet to explore, especially in Guatemala, where he has hiked the highlands, delved into the mysteries of the Ancient Maya, and surfed on the coast.

Russell is the author of *Culture Smart! Ecuador* (Gold Prize winner at the Pearl of the Pacific International Travel Journalism Awards at FITE in 2015), and *Culture Smart!* guides to Cuba, Mexico, Nicaragua, and Venezuela. He also wrote the *Bradt Guide to Venezuela*, and co-authored the most recent edition of the *Bradt Guide to Colombia*.

CONTENTS

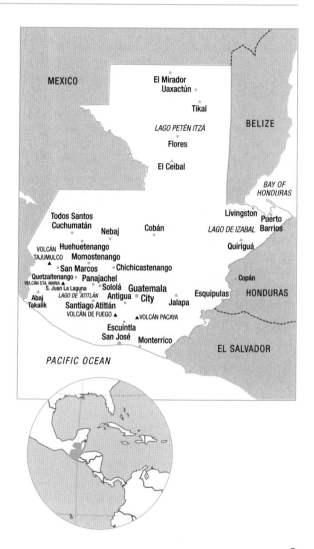

The third largest country in Central America and the second most populous, Guatemala is blessed with majestic Mayan ruins, cool cobblestoned colonial cities, smoking volcanoes, vast lakes, lush rainforests teeming with wildlife, mountainous forested highlands, and beaches along both its Caribbean and Pacific coasts.

The people are as diverse as the geography, with roughly half of Guatemalans identifying as indigenous Maya, a large population of Ladinos—the local word for the mixed Spanish and indigenous population—and a small but culturally significant population of Afro-Guatemalan Garífuna and indigenous Xinca.

Modern Guatemala still retains many elements of its ancient Maya past; but the clash of civilizations that occurred in 1523, when the Spanish conquistador Pedro de Alvarado defeated the king of the K'iche-Maya Tecún Umán at the battle of Xelajú, saw the Spanish crown, and later Ladino politicians, take over the reins of power.

That does not mean the Maya have given up their traditions. There are twenty-two distinct Maya languages spoken in Guatemala today, and the colorful blouses and skirts of the women, thriving markets, and full calendar of age-old fiestas attest to a commitment to conserve their indigenous identity, traditions, and customs.

The country has also been marked by the ferocious thirty-six-year civil war between right-wing governments and left-wing insurgents that ended in 1996 with the signing of a peace accord. The civil war led to many Guatemalans leaving their towns and villages and heading north to the US. That displacement continues today, fueled by economic hardship and the hope of providing their families with a better material future. Indeed, it was thanks to those Guatemalans who have made the journey to America sending home remittances that Guatemala was one of the only countries in the world whose economy did not shrink but rather grew during the coronavirus pandemic of 2020.

Despite their country's turbulent past, Guatemalans are resilient, family-focused, and hopeful for the future. They are welcoming and open to visitors who respect their culture.

Culture Smart! Guatemala provides an insight into the complexities of Guatemalan society. It dives deep into the country's history and describes the dynamics of daily life, the importance of family, how people socialize, and the cycle of indigenous and Catholic feasts and fiestas. It gives advice on building friendships and rapport with the people you'll meet, as well as tips on how to navigate a menu, which street food you should try, and how to travel around the country safely. For business travelers, there is a breakdown of the economy, and practical advice on how to navigate the local business world and avoid cultural misunderstandings.

Guatemala is a feast for the senses, and the best way to approach it is to slow down and do what the locals do. Useful phrases, both in Spanish and Mayan, are provided to help you to break the ice and make the most of your time in this beautiful and vibrant country.

Official Name	República de Guatemala	Republic of Guatemala
Population	18,500,000 (2025 est.)	The population growth rate is reducing annually.
Capital City	Ciudad de Guatemala	Pop. 1.3 million (city limits); 3 million (metropolitan area) 2025
Main Cities	Cobán (212,000), Quetzaltenango (180,000), Puerto Barrios (100,000), Chichicastenango (71,000), Antigua (46,000)	
Area	42,042 square miles (108,890 square km)	About the size of Bulgaria or the US state of Kentucky
Geography	Bordered by Mexico to the north, Belize to the east, Honduras and El Salvador to the south.	Guatemala has access to both the Atlantic Ocean in the east, and Pacific Ocean in the west.
Climate	Subtropical: Dry season Dec–April; Rainy season May–Nov	
Ethnic Makeup	Ladino (mixed indigenous and European descent) 56%; Indigenous 44% (2025 est.)	Guatemala has the largest indigenous Maya population in the world.
Language	Spanish is the official langauge. 22 Mayan languages are spoken countrywide.	Other languages spoken include Garífuna and Xinca.

Religion	Roman Catholic 45%; Protestants, Evangelicals, Jehovah's Witnesses 42%; Non-religious 11%; Small Jewish community	Many indigenous Guatemalans hold some traditional Maya spiritual beliefs and may engage in certain practices in addition to practicing Christianity.
Government	Democratic republic with president elected every four years; Unicameral Congress is made up of 160 deputies	
Media	Main newspapers: *Prensa Libre, El Periodico, Siglo 21, La Hora.* Tabloids: *Al Dia, Nuestro Diario*	Television: 26 broadcast channels including Canal 3 and Canal 5. Streaming services are available.
Currency	Quetzal (Q), divided into 100 centavos	The currency is named after the national bird.
GDP per Capita	US $4,596	The average GDP growth rate over the last decade was 3.6%, which is higher than the average for Central America.
Main Exports	Agricultural products including bananas, coffee, sugar, and greens	Other main exports include textiles, chemicals, and seafood.
Electricity	110 volts, 60HZ	European plugs need a Type A adapter with 2 flat prongs.
Telephone	International dialing code +502	
Time Zone	UTC/GMT -6 hours Central Standard Time	

CHAPTER ONE

LAND & PEOPLE

GEOGRAPHICAL SNAPSHOT

Guatemala, the northernmost of the Central American countries, is approximately 42,042 square miles (108,890 sq. km), making it about the size of the US state of Kentucky. It shares borders with its largest neighbor Mexico to the north, tiny Belize to the northeast, and Honduras and El Salvador to the southeast.

The country consists of three main regions: the temperate central highlands, with the heaviest population; the fertile tropical areas along the Pacific and Caribbean coasts; and the tropical jungle in the northern lowlands known as El Petén, which contains the famous Mayan site of Tikal.

In 2024 the national population was about 18.3 million, with an annual growth rate of about 1.2 percent. The capital, Guatemala City, has a population of about 3 million people. Other towns and cities include Escuintla, Cobán, Huehuetenango, Quetzaltenango, Antigua, Chichicastenango, and Puerto Barrios.

Guatemala is divided into twenty-two administrative *departamentos*, each of which has its own distinct cultural heritage and traditions. Huehuetenango— sometimes referred to as the "back door" of Guatemala, because political leaders would often flee through it to Mexico to escape political strife—is the most ethnically diverse department, with seven languages spoken. Within it sits the municipality of Todos Santos, in the Cuchumatàn mountains. Todos Santos is home to the Mam-speaking Maya, and is said to have one of the most magnificent views in all of Central America.

Quetzaltenango Department takes its name from the city of Quetzaltenango, which means "place of Quetzals" in Nahuatl, the language of the Tlaxcalan warriors from present-day Mexico who accompanied Pedro de Alvarado during the conquest of the region. Confusingly for foreign visitors, locals refer to the city and department as Xelajú (pronounced "shay-la-hu"), or the shorter Xela (pronounced "shay-la"), which comes from its pre-conquest K'iche' Maya name. Quetzaltenango is the second-largest city in Guatemala, an important hub of Maya culture and weaving, and a popular spot for foreigners who want to study Spanish in a more authentic-feeling location than Antigua.

An even greater cultural contrast can be seen in Livingston, in the Caribbean coastal department of Izabal, which can only be reached by boat from Puerto Barrios or along the Rio Dulce. Hot and tropical, Livingston swings to reggae rhythms and the insistent beats of Afro-Indigenous drums, and is home to the Garífuna people, or Garinagu, sometimes referred to as the Black Caribs. The Garífuna have a remarkable story.

They trace their descent from a mingling of indigenous Caribs and Arawaks living on the island of Saint Vincent, and a group of African slaves who were shipwrecked on the island in the seventeenth century. After resisting British slavers for many years, the Garífuna were forcibly relocated to Roatán in Honduras in the eighteenth century and then spread along the Caribbean coast of Central America from Belize to Nicaragua.

Guatemala's wild frontier, the sparsely populated and densely rainforested region of El Petén, is located in the far north of the country and covers about a third of the nation's territory. Once the heart of the ancient Maya world, the Petén is scattered with the remnants of spectacular cities such as Tikal—once home to over fifty thousand souls—where sturdy stepped pyramids provide panoramic views over a lush rainforest that teems with jungle wildlife like jaguars and tapirs, and resounds with the throaty call of howler monkeys. The main entry point for visitors to Tikal is the regional capital of Flores on Lago de Petén Itzá, which can be reached from Guatemala City on a short flight.

The cultural, gastronomic, and business heart of the country is Guatemala City, or Guate (pronounced "wa-tey") to locals. The modern capital sits in the central highlands at 4,921 feet (1,500 meters) above sea level and is the largest city in Central America. It was founded in 1776 after the old capital of Antigua was partly destroyed by earthquakes. All commercial flights coming into and out of Guatemala land at La Aurora International Airport, which is just a ten-minute taxi ride from the Plaza de la Constitución, the historic center in Zone 1. Although rush-hour traffic gridlock is a problem in

The town of San Juan La Laguna on the southern shore of Lake Atitlán.

some areas, Guatemala City has fine museums and galleries in Zone 1, a vibrant bar and nightlife scene in the Zona Viva area of Zone 10, and shiny new shopping malls and fine-dining restaurants in upmarket neighborhoods such as Zone 4 and Zone 14.

The country has both Pacific and Caribbean coasts and is located on the Pacific Ring of Fire, a tectonic belt of volcanoes and earthquake activity that stretches for about 25,000 miles (40,000 km) around the Pacific Ocean.

Three tectonic plates on the earth's crust meet in Guatemala, and the occasional grinding of those plates is the cause of the country's earthquakes. The plates are also responsible for producing Guatemala's thirty-seven official volcanoes. Many are extinct but eight are considered active, and the Pacaya, Fuego, and Santiaguito volcanoes are almost constantly active.

Reaching a lofty 14,507 feet (4,422 m) above sea level, the extinct Volcán Tajumulco is the country's tallest peak as well as the highest mountain in Central America, offering views from the summit into Mexico.

The short Caribbean coastline is susceptible to hurricanes and other tropical storms.

CLIMATE

Guatemala has been described as "The Land of Eternal Spring." This name comes from the springlike moderate climate that lasts year round.

There are two seasons: the dry season, from November (inland) or January (along the coast) to April; and the wet season, from May to October (inland) or December (along the coast). The coasts are hot and humid, with heavy rain during the wet season, although there is some decrease in humidity during the dry season. During the wet season it stays damp, with occasional downpours. The highlands have less rainfall and are cooler at night. Temperatures vary with altitude, ranging from an annual average of 77° to 86°F (25° to 30°C) on the coast, to 68°F (20°C) in the central highlands, and 59°F (15°C) in the higher mountains.

December and January are the coolest months, and in some areas there may even be snow on the mountaintops. Overall, however, Guatemala enjoys warm or hot days and cool evenings year round.

THE MAYA

The Maya are the largest American Indian group in North and Central America. Today, most Maya, about 5 million, live in Guatemala. The rest live in southern Mexico, Belize, and the western parts of El Salvador and Honduras. Strictly speaking, the term "Maya" refers to a historic grouping of languages, much like the Romance languages; today the word has come to represent the ethnic rights movement of the Maya people in Guatemala.

Guatemala is home to the largest indigenous population in Central America, and it's important to understand the difference between Maya and Ladinos. The Maya population in Guatemala is actually comprised of twenty-two distinct Mayan language groups, including the Achi', Akatec, Awakatec, Chalchitec, Ch'orti', Chuj, Itzá, Ixil, Jacaltec, Kaqchikel, K'iche', Mam, Mopan, Poqomam, Poqomchí, Q'anjob'al, Q'eqchí, Sakapultec, Sipakapense, Tektitek, Tz'utujil, and Uspantek. The Xinca are a small non-Maya indigenous group.

The largest Maya group is the K'iche', with a population of about 1.7 million, mainly concentrated in the highland departments of El Quiché (65.1 percent K'iche'), Totonicapán (95.9 percent), Quetzaltenango (25.9 percent), and Sololá (35.3 percent). The second biggest groups are the Mam, with five hundred thousand speakers in the departments of Quetzaltenango, Huehuetenango, San Marcos, and Retalhuleu.

There are roughly four hundred and fifty thousand speakers of Kaqchikel, which has linguistic similarities to K'iche' and Tz'utujil. The Kaqchikel heartland covers the departments of Guatemala, Sacatepéquez, Chimaltenango,

Maya women in *traje tipico*, traditional indigenous clothing.

and Sololá. A program to promote the teaching of
Kaqchikel in schools has seen a rise in the number of
speakers, while more recently, the talented Kaqchikel
singer Sara Curruchich from San Juan Comalapa has
helped promote indigenous pride as she takes her
distinctive brand of Kaqchikel and Spanish pop rock
and protest ballads to an international audience.

Certain areas of Guatemala are highly populated
by Maya groups. For example, Alta Verapaz is almost
100 percent Maya, and Sololá and San Marcos are
about 80 percent.

Certain areas of Guatemala are highly populated
by the Maya. For example, Alta Verapaz is almost
100 percent Maya, and Sololá and San Marcos are
about 80 to 85 percent.

The modern Maya of Guatemala consider themselves

the heirs of the ancient Maya cultures that once ruled these lands and traded, fought, and forged shifting alliances among themselves. After the Spanish conquest, many of these distinct linguistic groups were relocated in *reducciones* (literally "reductions"), towns and villages organized around a church, following a traditional Spanish model. The geographic isolation of these towns and villages, the strong kinship ties between extended families, and a tradition of marrying within the group helped to preserve Maya languages, customs, and traditional dress. In larger communities where different indigenous groups live side by side with Ladinos, some Maya have abandoned traditional dress, especially men. Ethnic discrimination against indigenous people has played a part in this, with some Maya parents choosing to adopt Spanish in the home to help their children get ahead. However, the continued existence of such a diversity of languages in the face of this pressure is a tribute to the deeply held pride among Maya speakers in their ancestral culture, and a commitment to preserving their languages into the future.

Today, the Maya are struggling to retain their cultural and ethnic identity, and have organized various activist groups in order to preserve their culture (such as, for example, the Aso Trama Maya women's weaving cooperative). Locally, Maya activists call this *el movimiento Maya* (the Maya Movement), while others have referred to it as Maya nationalism, the pan-Maya movement, and the Maya revitalization movement.

Other groups in Guatemala include the Xinca, who are indigenous non-Maya, and the Garífuna, who are African-Guatemalans living on the Caribbean coast of the country, with an ambiguous history regarding their origin.

100% CHAPÍN

Central Americans have some unusual names for themselves. Nicaraguans are Pinoleros, Hondurans are Catrachos, and Guatemalans refer to themselves as Chapínes. The name dates back to the Spanish Empire, when Antigua was the most important city in Central America and the administrative capital of the Captaincy General of Guatemala, which controlled all of present-day Central America apart from Panama.

One theory is that in the mid-seventeenth century, noble women of fashion in Spain would wear wooden or cork shoes with a leather inner sleeve that would make a distinctive chap-chap sound as they walked. Called *gachupines* or *cachupines*, the name of these fancy shoes came to be associated with the Spanish settlers who came out to the New World colonies to make their fortunes, and was a satirical way of ridiculing their foppish airs and graces. As the seat of power and wealth in Central America, Guatemala was seen as the home of the cachupines, and over time became the land of the chapínes, a name that was readily adopted by the locals.

Whatever the truth of the story, the majority of those who identify as Guatemaltecos are proud to be called Chapínes.

LADINOS

Mestizos of mixed European and indigenous ancestry
are known as "Ladinos," or locally as Guatemaltecos.
The name "Ladinos" comes from Latinos, and was
originally used to identify Spanish-speaking Maya who
adopted European ways and gave up traditional *traje*
(dress) and customs. It later extended to cover the new
post-conquest population created as Europeans and
Africans came to settle in these lands. Nowadays,
Ladinos refers to any non-indigenous Guatemalans.

Whether a person is Maya or Ladino really depends
on self-identification. Most Guatemalans actually
have a mix of Maya and Spanish bloodlines, with
only a few "purebloods" at each end of the spectrum.

Most Ladinos refer to themselves simply as
"Guatemalans" and generally live in urban centers,
although there are poor, rural Ladino villages as well.
Ladinos tend to dress in North American or European
style, speak Spanish, and typically reject their Maya
heritage, regarding it as inferior.

A BRIEF HISTORY

Earliest People

The long-held theory that hunter-gatherers from Siberia
populated the Americas after crossing the Bering Strait
at the end of the last Ice Age, around 11,500 years ago,
has been largely revised. Human footprints preserved in
volcanic ash in Valsequillo, Mexico, can be dated back
thirty-five thousand years, and other archeological finds

across the Americas suggest humans were here even earlier. Recent DNA research on indigenous groups indicates that the Americas were probably populated in several different waves of migration over many millennia. It's also probable that some of the first Americans used small boats to travel along the coast as they settled this New World.

The oldest dates for early hunter-gatherers living in present-day Guatemala are from ten thousand years ago, linked to stone tools and finely worked obsidian arrowheads found in the Guatemalan highlands, but archeologists expect new evidence will push those dates back further. Settlement and the forming of larger communities only came about nine thousand years ago, after the domestication of maize from teosinte, a wild grass growing in Central Mexico. Maize was first cultivated in the Maya lowlands around 6,500 years ago, and by 4,700 years ago had become a daily staple.

The Early Maya Pre-Classic Period (c. 1800 BCE –250 CE)

Maya civilization flourished in Guatemala during the first millennium CE. Then, mysteriously, it declined. Exactly what happened and why the Maya disappeared from various parts of Guatemala, Mexico, and Belize is unclear.

From excavations of ancient sites, we have learned that the early Maya settled in the central lowlands of the Petén between 2000 and 1500 BCE. The development of pottery and architecture in the Middle Preclassic period (c. 1000–300 BCE) shows the influence of the large Olmec civilization that originated in Veracruz, Mexico.

The Temple of the Great Jaguar at the Maya ruins of Tikal.

Then, in the Late Preclassic period (c. 300 BCE–250 CE), starting from about 1 CE there was an explosion of Maya culture in Guatemala, with the building of pyramids and temples at Tikal, Uaxactún, and other cities in the Petén and around the country. One of the greatest pre-classic Maya cities is Kaminaljuyu, near Guatemala City. Later Maya civilizations were noted for great cultural achievements, including hieroglyphic writing, knowledge of astronomy, architecturally designed cities, painted temples, stone monuments erected to honor important people, and other artistic forms such as painted ceramics and carved jade.

Maya Achievements

Before the Spanish conquest, Maya civilization dominated Central America. This was an extremely sophisticated and complex culture, with noteworthy achievements in architecture, agriculture, calendrics, astronomy, writing, and religion.

The ruins of the Maya sites testify to the grandeur and impressiveness of their civilization. One visit to Tikal is all one needs to understand the scale of their architectural greatness. Maya architecture was based on pyramidal bodies, incorporating elaborate, lengthy staircases and wide-open spaces, the positioning often based on astronomical observations.

In agriculture, the Maya moved away from slash-and-burn methods to more refined techniques of terracing, drainage, and irrigation, which improved the fertility of the soil and the retention of needed water. They are credited with domesticating corn, and consequently are sometimes referred to as the "people of the corn." The Maya also discovered vanilla beans, *frijoles* (beans), *chicle* (chewing gum), tobacco, and chocolate, among other products.

The Maya were obsessed with time. They developed elaborate calendar systems using astronomy and mathematics to understand and predict future events. The basis of calculation was a numerical system based on the number twenty, and deities were assigned to represent the numbers one to twenty in the calendrical system.

In astronomy, the Maya were interested in the solar year, the lunar cycle, and movements of the planets. They were able to calculate all of these with astonishing accuracy compared to current calculations. They developed a highly sophisticated and artistic hieroglyphic writing, which in its style and use of pictures distinguishes it from other cultures of ancient Mesoamerica.

Alongside the development of sciences and architecture, the Maya had an elaborate theory of the origin of the world, the shape of the universe, and the deities living in it. Maya cosmology is characterized by balance, layers, and opposites, and they believed in cycles of creation and destruction. According to the Maya, the Earth is a flat surface, with four corners each associated with a particular color. They thought of the flat Earth as the back of a giant crocodile relaxing in a pool of water lilies, and the sky as a double-headed serpent. They believed that there were many layers in the sky and that the four corners of the sky were supported by four trees of different colors and species, with a great Ceiba (silk cotton) tree at its center. Above the sky existed a heaven composed of thirteen layers, each with its own god. In this conception, the top layer was overseen by a type of screech owl, the Muan bird, and the gloomy underworld (Xibalda) of nine layers was seen to be the destination after death.

The Maya believed in more than one hundred and
sixty deities, each of whom had variable manifestations
(opposite sex, underworld counterparts, different ages,
and so on). There is some evidence of a single supreme
deity called Itzamná. A patrilineal line of Maya priests
were in charge of calendars, festivals, ceremonies, rituals,
divination, healing, writing, and learning. During most
rituals, Maya engaged in bloodletting of themselves and
their captives in order to anoint religious articles, and as
an offering to the gods. Animal and human sacrifices were
also often performed. Copal resin was (and still is) almost
always burned during Maya rituals. Today, many Maya
believe that mountains are places where deities dwell,
and their ancient temple-pyramids were essentially man-
made mountains in honor of those deities. Caves were
considered the entrance to Xibalba, the Maya underworld
where the gods of the dead lived. Traditional Maya
shamans still pray and leave offerings at mountain shrines
and in caves. There is also a continuing belief in the spirits
of the forest, and evil winds that can provoke illness and
disease in the world.

The Classic Maya Period (c. 250–900 CE)

According to many archeologists, Maya culture was at
its zenith during this period. This was when the Maya
developed the famous Long Count calendar and a
recognizable form of writing. There was a marked
increase in temple, altar, and monument construction,
and increased military conquest.

At the apex of Maya society was the semi-divine king,
and below him a large, sophisticated royal court. Nobles

Eighth-century Maya engraving found at the dig site known as La Corona.

ran smaller fiefdoms on his behalf, and a wealthy upper class surfaced due to the growth in long-distance trade. Status was displayed by jewelry and adornment. One of the most valuable commodities was chocolate: cocoa beans were used as currency, and the nobility drank the cocoa. At the base of society were the peasants who worked the maize fields and lived in the forests.

The Maya seemed to organize themselves with and trade among a federation of city-states, each with their own religion and culture. Warfare became common, with city-states vying for power.

The Maya in Decline

After about 830 CE, the elaborate construction and material advances of the Classic period came to a halt. Although the reason is not known, there are many theories about what caused the decline of the Maya population. Some believe that the great Maya city-states succumbed to the general conflict and disorder common throughout Mesoamerica; others posit that a peasant revolt may have broken out in response to the growth and unreasonable demands of the ruling elite. Some scholars point to overpopulation and a demand for increased food production, and the subsequent loss of soil fertility and environmental problems. Epidemics, widespread illnesses, droughts, and other natural disasters may also have contributed to the decline and collapse of the Maya cities.

By about the tenth century, Maya culture began to die out in many of their previously well-populated areas in Guatemala. As the Maya abandoned their city-states, the majority moved to northern Belize, the Yucatán Peninsula, and the Guatemalan highlands to the south, where they developed small rural villages with terraced farming and irrigation. Today, this area of Guatemala still has standing ruins and monuments from the Classic period, and the indigenous people who live there are proud of the Maya traditions.

Preconquest: The Highland Tribes

Toward the end of the thirteenth century the Toltecs, an extremely militaristic tribe from northern Mexico, invaded the central Guatemalan highlands and dramatically changed the Maya way of life. They created a much more secular and aggressive society based on military rule. The Toltecs as the ruling elite of the area founded a series of competing empires around Guatemala that began the fragmentation of the Maya into distinct tribal groups. The largest of these empires was the K'iche', who were dominant in the central area of Guatemala and later expanded their power base by conquering less powerful tribes. In 1475 when Quicab, the great K'iche' ruler behind the conquest, died, the empire suffered from lack of authority and power. For the next fifty or so years, all the tribes continued to be in conflict, fighting over inadequate resources and the lack of available land.

The Spanish Conquest

The Spanish arrived in Guatemala to find much chaos and crisis, which they were able to exploit to their advantage. The Spanish adventurer Pedro de Alvarado had taken part in the conquest of Mexico with Cortés. He was dispatched from Mexico with an army of Spaniards and Mexican Tlaxcalans, who had allied themselves with Cortés

during the Mexican conquest. He arrived in Guatemala in 1523 and quickly became known as one of the most evil, cruel, and rapacious conquistadores of his time. On a quest for gold and other profitable goods, Alvarado defeated most of the major Maya tribes in Guatemala; only the ferocious Achi in the Verapaces— known as the Land of War (Tierra de Guerra)—held his

Bartolomé de las Casas.

armies at bay. This area was eventually won over by Dominican missionaries led by Bartolomé de las Casas, the first Christian activist for the rights of native peoples, which earned it its name of Verapaz ("true peace").

On his hunt for treasure and riches, Alvarado traveled to Peru, then back to Guatemala, and then was called in to quell a revolt in Mexico, meeting his death after being crushed by a horse that slipped and fell on top of him.

WHY "GUATEMALA?"

There is a lively debate over how "Guatemala" got its name. The first time it ever appeared in writing is in a letter that the conquistador Pedro de Alvarado penned on April 11, 1524 to Hernán Cortés in Mexico, in which he said "the city of Guatemala" had sent warriors to assist him. Alvarado was referring to the fortress capital of the Maya-speaking Kakchiquel people, who called the city Iximché.

There are several theories as to why Alvarado used the name Guatemala and not Iximché, but the most probable is that it comes from *Cuauhtemallan* (Place of Many Trees), which is the name the Tlaxcallan warriors who accompanied Alvarado from Mexico would have called Iximché in their native Nahuatl. (Iximché in Mayan literally means "maize tree.") Other translators have come up with "rotten wood," but "place of many trees" is the most likely.

Spanish Colonial Rule

The conquest of Guatemala did not bring immediate
wealth to the Spanish conquistadors who settled here, as
there were few treasures of gold and silver compared to
the ones plundered from the Aztec Empire in Mexico or
the Incas in Peru.

The rewards were land and laborers, and the Spaniards
immediately set up a system of *encomiendas*, which
granted seized Maya lands and the people who lived on
them to Spanish colonizers. Scattered Maya communities
were gathered into Spanish-style towns and villages
known as *reducciones* (reductions), each of which had a
church and a marketplace at its center. Indigenous people
were effectively treated as slaves, working for free and
producing crops for their new masters and the church.
Many Maya fled to the mountains or the rainforest to
escape the *reducciones* and many thousands died from
Western diseases against which they had no immunity.

It was at this time that Maya villages developed their
distinctive *trajes*, with particular colors and symbols
woven into their traditional clothing. Some believe that
the Spanish used *traje* as a means of identifying Maya
from specific villages, while others believe that the *traje*
naturally developed in each village as a result of local
creativity. The reality is probably somewhere in between.

With a new social structure forced on them, the Maya
began organizing themselves politically and socially in
these new villages and found ways to maintain their
traditions alongside the colonial hierarchy and Catholic
power structures that predominated.

By the early nineteenth century, over three centuries
of colonial rule had completely transformed Guatemala,

with the creation of hundreds of new villages and two big cities, the imposition of the Catholic faith, and an economy based on the export of cash crops like cacao, cotton, and indigo. Society was highly stratified, with the indigenous Maya at the bottom, Ladinos above them, and a small, extremely wealthy ruling Spanish elite at the top.

Independence

In the early 1800s, Spain turned its gaze away from its American colonies as domestic matters took center-stage with Napoleon's invasion of the Iberian Peninsula in 1808. The resulting adoption of a liberal constitution in Spain in 1812 led to reform in the Spanish colonies, but also to growing demands for independence from the burden of taxation and the rule of distant Spain. The conflict saw the emergence of two distinct groups in Central and South America—the liberals (in favor of a secular and more egalitarian state) and the conservatives (supporting the Church and the Crown).

The Captaincy-General of Guatemala, which covered the modern Central American states of Guatemala, El Salvador, Honduras, Nicaragua, and Costa Rica, and the Mexican state of Chiapas, was governed between 1811 to 1818 by José de Bustamante y Guerra, and his strong military response to put down any revolts—and a general fear from Ladinos and Creoles that an indigenous uprising would threaten their existence too—averted the kind of revolutionary independence wars that erupted throughout Mexico and South America.

Instead, on September 15, 1821, a provincial council in Guatemala City signed an official document known as the Acta de Independencia Centroamericana (Central

American Independence Act), which proclaimed the independence of Central America from the Spanish Empire. The problem for this fledgling entity was that the provincial powers could not agree on their future. Some of the provinces favored joining Mexico, while others favored a Central American confederation under a federal system like the US, with Guatemala as the administrative center. After a brief stint of being annexed by Mexico, The United Provinces of Central America was formed in 1823 as a federal republic made up of Guatemala, El Salvador, Honduras, Nicaragua, and Costa Rica. Revolts and uprisings by the Maya, who felt left out and wanted change from oppressive Spanish power structures still in place, resulted in a peasant rebellion led by Guatemala's Rafael Carrera that defeated the forces of Francisco Morazán in 1840, effectively ending the federation. On March 21, 1847, Guatemala declared itself an independent republic, and Carrera became its first president.

The Coffee Boom

German settlers arriving in Guatemala in the 1860s and 1870s set up coffee plantations in the highland departments of Alta Verapaz and Quetzaltenango, quickly establishing themselves as major players in the coffee business and making coffee the country's most important export crop.

The establishment of coffee coincided with a period that started with the Liberal Revolution of 1871 and the overthrow of General Vicente Cerna, led by Miguel García Granados and Justo Rufino Barrios, who became president in 1873. Rufino Barrios modernized Guatemala by establishing a national bank, developing ports, and extending the railway network in order to capitalize on the country's coffee boom.

For the Maya, the boom meant more of their land was confiscated by the government and converted into coffee plantations, and they were then forced to work on the plantations, especially during the seasonal harvest from late November to April and early May.

The Era of the Banana Empire

President Barrios was killed in 1885 while fighting for a unified Central America, and Manuel Estrada Cabrera, an authoritarian ruler who supported big businesses, assumed dictatorial powers in Guatemala. Cabrera is noted for having the longest one-man rule in Central American history. He was instrumental in encouraging additional railway expansion and foreign investment, in particular with the US-based United Fruit Company, known as El Pulpo (The Octopus), such was the power and influence it wielded in Guatemala as a banana monopoly.

With the election of Jorge Ubico as president in 1931, the United Fruit Company became the dominant force in Guatemala, with even more power than the government; it invested great amounts of capital in the country, bought significant shares in the railroad, electric utility, and telegraph companies, and owned over 40 percent of the land.

Ubico ruled the country with an iron fist. He suppressed all political and intellectual opposition and continued to exploit the indigenous Maya, subjecting them completely to the state. He introduced an anti-vagrancy law that required Maya to carry a passbook proving they had worked 100–150 days a year, without pay, on the large estates or on public projects implemented by him. Without this proof, they could be put in jail or worse.

Ubico eventually became paranoid, developing an obsessive identification with the military during his thirteen-year reign. It's said that he saw himself as the reincarnation of Napoleon, and kept pictures of Napoleon around himself. He had a large spy network, was heavily guarded, and severely punished any dissent by incarceration or death. As Ubico's regime grew more repressive, student and labor demonstrations and revolts increased. In 1944, he was forced to resign by the October Revolutionaries, a group of disenchanted military officers, students, and professionals, following the example of other popular uprisings against dictatorships in Central and South America.

Ten Years of Spring Ends with CIA Coup

After Ubico's overthrow, a provisional government ruled the country for almost two years before democratic elections in 1945 saw a progressive and democratic intellectual, Juan José Arévalo, elected president. A former professor, he was able to institute social, educational, and health reforms, and was instrumental in giving land rights back to the Maya people. His presidency started "The Ten Years of Spring," a period of free speech and political diversity, attempts at land reform, and an ethos of progress across the country.

The next president, Jacobo Arbenz, continued in the same vein by taking on land reform and the biggest business monopoly in Guatemala, the United Fruit Company. In 1952 Arbenz instituted the Law of Agrarian

Reform, by which unused or state-owned land would be distributed to the landless. This infuriated the United Fruit Company (and the US's other commercial interests in Guatemala), long accustomed to doing as it pleased under previous governments, leading it to spread rumors of communist infiltration in the Arbenz administration. At the time, John Foster Dulles, the US Secretary of State, and his brother Allen Dulles, the director of the Central Intelligence Agency (CIA),

Juan José Arévalo.

were on the board of the United Fruit Company and feared a fall in profits if Arbenz continued progressive

Diego Rivera's 1954 mural *Gloriosa victoria*, depicting the CIA and the United Fruit Company.

land reforms. They falsely painted the center-left Arbenz as a communist threat to the US, and President Eisenhower authorized the CIA to arm and fund a force led by Guatemalan Colonel Carlos Castillo Armas to overthrow him. The 1982 book *Bitter Fruit: The Story of an American Coup in Guatemala* by Stephen Schlesinger and Stephen Kinzer is a comprehensive account of the CIA's operation in Guatemala, which has also been tackled in fictional form by the Peruvian Nobel-winning author Mario Vargas Llosa in his 2019 novel *Harsh Times*.

Military Rule

Colonel Carlos Castillo Armas became president in 1954 and immediately began a crackdown on left-wing sympathizers, labor leaders, and student activists. His assassination in 1957 brought a period of violence and unrest.

Many left-leaning organizers and non-political Maya were killed during this unstable time. In 1960, a group of junior military officers, inspired by the Cuban Revolution, tried to overthrow the government, but failed. This group then formed the base of the guerrilla movement that along with other groups fought the Guatemalan government for the next thirty-six years. As the fighting between the left-wing guerrillas and the US-supported military government of Guatemala grew more intense and bloody, the economy declined and migration soared.

The worst of the bloodshed occurred during the presidency of retired general Efraín Ríos Montt who came to power in 1982 following a coup d'état. Ríos Montt introduced a scorched-earth policy, part of a counterinsurgency campaign that—in the search for guerrillas and to eradicate any support they might find in the countryside—resulted in the massacre of entire Maya Indian villages.

Rigoberta Menchú.

Although violent executions, tortures, and forced disappearances were carried out by both sides, the majority of the atrocities (estimated at 93 percent by the 1999 truth commission) were committed by the government-run military and civil defense patrols under the military's control. It's estimated that some 626 Maya villages in the highlands of Guatemala were destroyed, and approximately one hundred thousand Maya Indians lost their lives at the hands of the Guatemalan military. At the same time, numerous Maya women and girls were raped and murdered, and many Maya fled to the mountains and jungles or went into exile in neighboring countries, especially Mexico, where many still live today.

Some describe this violent history as genocide, the attempted eradication of the Maya people. A K'iche' woman, Rigoberta Menchú, survived among the deaths of many family members. She gives an account of what happened to her and her community during the civil war in her book *I, Rigoberta Menchú*. In 1992, she won the

Nobel Peace Prize for her work for social justice and the rights of indigenous peoples.

These years were a terrifying time for most Guatemalans, especially for those who publicly opposed and exposed repression and advocated reform.

Return to Democracy

Ríos Montt was ousted by his defense minister, General Mejía Victores, in a coup in 1983, just one year after originally taking power. An amnesty was declared for the guerrillas and a new constitution was adopted in 1985. It established an independent judiciary and a human rights ombudsman, and made way for Vinicio Cerezo Arévelo to

be elected president— the first democratically elected leader since 1966. Cerezo tried to end political violence and establish the rule of law, confining the military to providing security for the state. Although there was a decrease in violence and the economy improved at the beginning of his presidency, he did not prosecute human-rights violations vigorously, and he failed to deal with

Pro-democracy demonstration.

major problems such as infant mortality, illiteracy, poor health and social services, and resurgent political violence involving both the army and the guerrillas.

In 1991 Jorge Serrano Elías was elected president, the first civilian to succeed a previous civilian president. Under Serrano, civil unrest grew. He suspended the constitution, dissolved Congress and the Supreme Court, and censored the press, incurring both domestic and international opposition and inspiring the freezing of most foreign aid. Serrano was deposed and a return to constitutional rule was promised by Congress.

Ramiro de León Carpio was then elected as president, which gave much hope to the country as he had previously been the human rights ombudsman under both Arévelo and Serrano. He hoped to put an end to government corruption and violence, but this hope was short-lived, as human-rights violations continued and many communities took the law into their own hands because they perceived the government to be failing.

Toward Peace

Despite the issues in De León's administration, the peace process took on new life, especially when the United Nations became involved. Agreements were signed on human rights, indigenous rights, resettlement of displaced persons, and historical clarification. The rebels agreed to a ceasefire.

Alvaro Arzú followed De León in the presidency and concluded the peace negotiations. In December 1996, with the support of the UN, the government signed peace accords with the leftist insurgents, the Unidad Revolucionaria Nacional Guatemalteca, thus ending the thirty-six-year civil war in Guatemala. The peace accords called for a reduction in size of the Guatemalan army and the demobilization of the rebel forces. Arzú and his administration also took steps to reduce military influence in civil affairs and improve human rights.

Alfonso Portillo was elected to office beginning in January 2000, and promised to uphold the peace accords, reform the military, and investigate human-rights violations. Portillo was criticized by many because of the continued influence of Ríos Montt (then the head of Congress) in his decisions. Scandal, corruption, a faltering economy, and crime plagued most of Portillo's presidency.

Corruption, Covid, and Change

Guatemala entered the twenty-first century with the presidency of Alfonso Portillo. Hope for change was short-lived as scandals, government corruption, high crime rates, human-rights violations, and a faltering economy led to growing public unrest. Violent demonstrations erupted in Guatemala City in 2003 as Ríos Montt's supporters took to the streets demanding that a ban on him running for president be overturned, even though he was a former coup leader. In the end, Ríos Montt was able to stand but came third in the first round of voting, and Óscar Berger of the liberal reform Grand Alliance for National Unity political party was elected president.

Portillo, meanwhile, fled to Mexico to avoid charges that he had stolen money from the armed forces. Eventually, he was extradited from Guatemala to the US and sentenced to a little under six years in jail, after he pleaded guilty to accepting bribes from Taiwan in exchange for a promise that his country would continue to recognize Taiwan diplomatically.

The two decades since Óscar Berger's presidency have seen the UN set up a program in Guatemala to tackle corruption, president after president indicted on corruption charges, the devastating effects of hurricanes like Stan in 2005 and Eta and Iota in 2020, and the tragic loss of lives following a slow government response to the Covid-19 pandemic.

The high point of Berger's presidency was the signing of the Central American Free Trade Agreement (CAFTA-DR), a free trade area similar to the NAFTA that includes the US, Guatemala, El Salvador, Honduras, Nicaragua, Costa Rica, and the Dominican Republic. He also oversaw the creation of the International Commission Against Impunity in Guatemala (CICIG) in 2006, an independent international body set up by the United Nations to help the Public Prosecutor's Office and the National Civil Police to root out endemic corruption in government, state bodies, and security forces.

Berger's successor, President Álvaro Colom, had bold plans to improve the conditions of Guatemala's indigenous communities and improve education, but was almost immediately sucked into a series of scandals and corruption allegations that followed him after his presidency.

A former general who had served as Director of Military Intelligence, Otto Pérez Molina, who followed Colom, was elected with a pledge to bring a *mano dura* (strong hand) against crime, but never finished his mandate. Both Pérez Molina and his vice president, Roxana Baldetti, resigned after a customs racket known as La Linea that let businesses avoid import taxes in return for bribes was exposed, sparking mass protests. Both were later prosecuted on corruption charges.

Outrage over government corruption saw a protest vote in the 2015 presidential elections that brought TV comedian Jimmy Morales a landslide victory in the second round. Campaigning with the slogan *Ni corrupto, ni ladrón* (Neither corrupt, nor a thief), Morales promised to clean up government, but was soon mired in his own scandals when his brother Sammy and one of his sons were charged with corruption and money laundering. After the CICIG opened an investigation into his campaign finances and other irregularities, Morales responded by banning the Colombian prosecutor heading the CICIG from returning to Guatemala, effectively shutting down the CICIG.

In 2020, the presidency of Alejandro Giammattei had barely started when the Covid-19 pandemic broke out and a state of calamity was declared by Congress, leading to measures such as social distancing, the closure of shopping malls and restaurants, transport restrictions, and a nightly curfew. With over 70 percent of the working population engaged in the informal economy, furlough schemes did little to address the financial hardships of people who lived day to day from what they earned. The government's slow action on disbursing funding for the hardest hit saw the army drawn in to deliver food parcels. By May 2020, enforced lockdowns saw Guatemalans coming out on the streets with white flags to protest at the government's response and indicate that they had no food or provisions. After the pandemic, public schools started to reopen in March 2022, and all entry restrictions to Guatemala were lifted in August.

Giammattei, like many of his predecessors, faced corruption allegations while in office, and his attorney general María Consuelo Porras was accused of blocking corruption investigations when she dismissed the head of the Special Prosecutor's Office against impunity. In 2021, the US Department of State added her to its list of "undemocratic and corrupt" officials.

The surprise victory of sociologist and diplomat Bernardo Arévalo in the 2023 presidential election showed how deeply Guatemalans wanted change and an end to entrenched government corruption. The son of former President Juan José Arévalo, who was democratically elected in 1945 after the fall of the Ubico dictatorship, Bernardo Arévalo promised to root out corruption and introduce progressive social reforms to address economic and social inequality affecting indigenous communities in the highlands. All through the election and after, Arévalo and his Movimiento Semilla (Seed) party faced relentless legal challenges from Attorney General Porras, aimed at derailing Arévalo's campaign and invalidating his election victory. It was only after thousands of students and indigenous protesters took to the streets for weeks in Guatemala, and strong international demands that the democratic process be respected from the US, OAS, and EU, that Arévalo was sworn in. Nobody in Guatemala expects an instant solution to the long-running problem of corruption, but Arévalo's inauguration has given hope to indigenous rights' campaigners that a more equitable distribution of government funding can improve healthcare provision, and work and education opportunities, for the poorest.

NATIONAL SYMBOLS

The **national flag** of Guatemala features two vertical stripes of sky blue with a central stripe in white that includes the national coat of arms, with a resplendent quetzal resting atop of a scroll marking the date of Central American independence, September 15, 1821. Known as the *Azul y Blanco* for its colors, the design was only adopted officially in 1871, on the date's fiftieth anniversary.

National Anthem: "¡Guatemala feliz...!" (Merry Guatemala), written in 1897 by Cuban poet and diplomat José Joaquín Palma, has some really bloodthirsty lyrics and was toned down in 1934 by the Guatemalan poet José María Bonilla Ruano, on the orders of the dictator General Jorge Ubico Castañeda. In English, the first verse is: "Merry Guatemala...! That your altars never be profaned by the tormentor, nor there be slaves who lick the yoke, nor tyrants who spit on your face."

It's a crime in Guatemala to insult or vilify the flag, the national emblem, or the national anthem.

National Bird: Resplendent Quetzal (*Pharomachrus mocinno*).

National Flower: *La Monja Blanca* or White Nun orchid (*Lycaste virginalis*).

National Tree: Ceiba or kapok tree (*Ceiba pentandra*)—a tree sacred to the ancient and modern Maya, traditionally linking the sky or heaven with Xibalba, the underworld.

THE ECONOMY

Guatemala has the largest economy in Central America. Its GDP in 2024 was around US $110 billion, way above its closest neighbors Honduras and Beliz, which had GDPs of US $38 billion and US $3.5 billion respectively. The main driver of Guatemala's economic growth is the private sector, which includes service industries such as private health care, customer services, financial services, banking, communications, retail, and tourism. These generate the largest share of GDP—around 55 percent—and employ nearly half of the working population.

Tourism is one of the country's most important money earners and the fastest-growing sector of the economy, bringing in billions of dollars every year.

Manufacturing includes the production of coffee, textiles, paper, petroleum, pharmaceuticals, and rubber, and makes up about 15 percent of the economy.

Guatemala's largest trading partner is the United States, and in August 2004 it signed the Dominican Republic–Central America–United States Free Trade Agreement (CAFTA–DR) alongside the United States, the Dominican Republic, Costa Rica, El Salvador, Honduras, and Nicaragua.

Agricultural products like coffee, bananas, sugar, cotton and fruits used to be the backbone of the economy and one of the main sources of employment, but now represent less than 10 percent of GDP and employ about 25 percent of the population.

Guatemala is the largest exporter of cardamom in the world. A peppery spice native to India, it was first introduced to the cloud forests of Alta Verapaz in 1914 by German plantation owner Oscar Majus Kloeffer, who thought he could undercut the price of the spice produced in Kerala by growing it on his coffee plantation in Cobán. The cardamom grown today in Alta Verapaz is known locally as Oro Verde (Green Gold) and makes up about 70 percent of global production; although, like coffee, returns for the farmers are low.

Palm oil production has taken off in the last ten years, and Guatemala is one of the world's fastest-growing producers of it, ranking third in total exports after Indonesia and Malaysia. The downside is that the introduction of industrially farmed crops like palm oil has seen some of the country's most fertile lands turned over to intensive monoculture plantations, the diversion of water sources away from villages that depend on them,

Coffee beans being harvested by hand.

and the loss of the sustainable *milpa* farming method of growing maize, squash, and beans, which has barely changed since the days of the ancient Maya.

Guatemala is the fourth-largest producer of macadamia nuts in the world. Growing macadamia nut trees is preferential to "slash-and-burn" agriculture (cutting trees and burning dried brush, which in the long term depletes the soil) that is common across the country, because the trees replenish the soil and their leaves take up carbon dioxide while releasing oxygen.

REMITTANCES

Perhaps paradoxically, one of the biggest sectors of the economy is remittances, the money sent back by Guatemalans living and working abroad. It made up nearly 20 percent of GDP in 2024, and continues to grow year on year. Most of the money comes from the estimated 3 million Guatemalans living in the United States. Because of this, Guatemala was one of the few countries in the world that saw its economy grow during the Covid-19 pandemic, with remittances in 2021 increasing 35 percent compared to the previous year.

The unequal distribution of land and wealth, the meager wages paid to farm laborers, and the rising costs of imported food have made rural life increasingly difficult for indigenous and Ladino Guatemalans, and has served to widen existing wealth and health inequalities. It has also fueled the exodus of young men and women to the United States who see migration as the only future for their families.

There is a wide gap between the rich and the poor in Guatemala; the wealthiest 10 percent own more than half the country's wealth, while about 80 percent of the population live in poverty, and around two-thirds of those live in extreme poverty. Over 60 percent of the land is owned by less than 2 percent of the population. Wealthy landowners have always used cheap labor supplied by the Maya, and forced labor continued until the signing of the peace accords in 1996. Today, the Maya still work under harsh conditions and earn meager wages relative to their Ladino counterparts.

EMIGRATION

One consequence of the years of violence and civil war that destroyed hundreds of villages was the exodus of indigenous Maya and poor Ladino Guatemalans to Mexico and the United States. Fueled by poor wages and unemployment, that exodus continues today. While some Guatemalans are able to secure temporary visas to work in agriculture in the US, the majority must make a dangerous journey through Mexico in order to cross the American border. Those who succeed and are able to find a job are able to send money back to their family in Guatemala. According to figures from the Guatemalan Ministry of Foreign Affairs, there are an estimated 3 million Guatemalans residing in the United States.

Visit any highland town where family members have made the journey to the US for work and you will see the houses that have been built, the cars that have been purchased, and the many small businesses that have started as a result of wages earned abroad. The effect this has on local lives cannot be overstated; poor families will put children through school with this money, something they otherwise would be unable to do.

In the highland Mam-speaking town of Todos Santos Cuchumatan, where both men and women wear traje, people have been migrating to Oakland, California since the 1980s, and have created a tight-knit community of five thousand there in the Fruitvale District. That is quite extraordinary from a total population of just thirty-three thousand back in Todos Santos Cuchumatan. An indication of the importance that a US salary can have to a family's fortunes, in the cemetery in Todos Santos Cuchumatán many tombs are painted with the US stars and stripes, a custom that is repeated in other indigenous towns and villages like Chichicastenango. The rural village of Chivarreto, outside Qutzeltenango, is known locally as the Pequeno Hollywood de Guatemala (Guatemala's Little Hollywood), after migrant workers in Los Angeles sent money back to their hometown to erect large white letters spelling out the village's name on a hillside in the style of the famous Hollywood sign.

GOVERNMENT AND POLITICS

Guatemala is a constitutional democratic republic, with independent executive, legislative, and judicial branches of government. The executive is composed of the president, the vice president, secretaries of state, cabinet ministers, and vice ministers. The legislative body is the Congress, which has 158 deputies who are directly elected for four-year terms.

The judiciary is composed of the Corte de Constitucionalidad (Constitutional Court), the highest court in the land, and the Corte Suprema de Justicia (Supreme Court of Justice), which is the highest court of appeal in the country. There are also appeals courts, civil courts, and penal courts. Specialist courts deal with labor disputes, disputes of administrative litigation, conflicts of jurisdiction, military affairs, and other related concerns that are not governed by the ordinary courts. Trials are public, and defendants have the right to counsel, are presumed innocent until proven guilty, and can be released on bail.

The president is the head of state, prime minister, and commander-in-chief of the army. People who have been involved in a takeover or a *coup d'état* are ruled ineligible for the presidency, although the former dictator Ríos Montt challenged the law and was allowed to run for president in the 2003 elections. Both the president and the vice president are elected by popular vote and can serve only one four-year term.

The presidential elections of 2023 saw anti-corruption candidate Bernardo Arévalo of the Movimiento Semilla (Seed Movement) party win a surprise second-round victory with 61 percent of the vote. A center-left progressive, Arévalo is the son of Guatemala's first democratically elected president, Juan José Arévalo.

An attempt by the attorney general's office to overturn the election result on the grounds that the new party Movimiento Semilla had not been properly registered was thrown out by the electoral authorities and denounced as a political coup attempt by international observers, but fears that the governing elite would try to derail Arévalo's inauguration led to widespread demonstrations and roadblocks across the country. In the end, Arévalo was sworn in as the 52nd president of Guatemala on January 15th, 2024, but challenges to his government remain.

The twenty-two departments each have a governor who is appointed by the president, and the municipalities are governed by popularly elected mayors or councils.

For such a small country, Guatemala has many political parties, though gaining political power has mostly been due to the personal influence of the leader rather than that of any political organization. Due to the high number of parties, power sharing coalitions are common.

CHAPTER TWO

VALUES &
ATTITUDES

There is a clear divide between those living in traditional indigenous communities, such as the Maya and Ixil, and those who belong to the Spanish-speaking Ladino community, which makes it difficult to generalize about the values and attitudes of the Guatemalan people as though it were a monolithic entity. There is also a gulf that divides those Guatemalans who struggle to get by each day and the wealthy who live a life of air-conditioned luxury and country-club comforts. Cultural backgrounds, extremes of poverty and wealth, and a rural-urban divide all contribute to the range of attitudes you will encounter among the Guatemalans that you will meet.

And yet, despite their differences, there are common attitudes that are shared across the social divide. For example, all Guatemalans place great value on family ties, on maintaining a warm and congenial temperament, and on being respectful to those they interact with. Many also possess a sense of pride that can sometimes border on the sensitive, a laid-back attitude toward timekeeping, and a fondness for nicknames and terms of endearment that are used among friends and family.

The Guatemalan people can fairly be described as proud, hardworking, and vibrant, and visitors to the country can expect a warm and friendly reception.

RELIGION

All Guatemalans, both Ladinos and indigenous, have been shaped by the Christian religion, whether practicing or not. Nowadays, only 45 percent of the population identify as Catholic, and year on year that number is decreasing. And yet, the far-reaching influence of the Church persists. Its conversion of the indigenous population by Catholic priests began in 1524 with the arrival of Spanish conquistador Pedro de Alvarado. The impressive churches of Antigua, each one decorated with huge gilded altars and religious artworks, reflect the opulent wealth these institutions of moral instruction and social control once enjoyed.

Under colonial rule, the Church had a virtual monopoly over worship and education, including the right to tax all worshipers 10 percent of their income, and censoring what was published. The power of the Church continued until Guatemala became a secular state in 1821—and its power was again briefly reinstated between 1854 and 1871 by conservative leaders after the Papacy complained.

For many, Catholicism is something they are born into rather than a devout calling—and thus baptisms, first communions, confirmations, weddings, and funerals remain important milestones in people's lives. Even Guatemalans who don't go to church will carry images of saints and virgins for "protection," place a candle in front of a Catholic saint to say a prayer and ask a favor, or join a procession on the Catholic holidays.

In the highlands, the Maya have incorporated elements of their indigenous cosmovision with Catholic rituals and practices to create a syncretic form of folk Catholicism, where a prayer to the Virgin Mary may also invoke a Maya deity.

Catholic festivals and saints' days are not always as traditional as they are in Spain, and may reflect indigenous customs and beliefs from before the conquest. This is especially true in the highlands, and on days like All Saints Day, which coincides with the Maya celebration of the Day of the Dead (see Chapter 3).

Protestant and evangelical church groups such as Southern Baptists, the Church of Jesus Christ of Latter-day Saints (Mormons), Jehovah's Witnesses, and others have made inroads in poor areas of the big cities, especially in Guatemala City, and in indigenous areas in the highlands. There are hundreds of these churches, and they minister to about 40 percent of the population.

Evangelical Sects

Guatemala has seen the largest growth of evangelical Christianity in Latin America. According to the Evangelical General Council, the Alianza Evangelica, there are more than nineteen thousand Protestant churches in Guatemala representing more than ninety denominations, including Baptists, Nazarenes, and Guatemalan-created Pentecostal groups such as El Shaddai. The Assembly of God is the largest denomination, followed by the Church of God of the Complete Gospel. In recent years Protestant and evangelical missionaries have been competing for followers. Many have brought hope and practical assistance to rural villages—building houses and helping in the provision of food, medicine, and education— and have gained many converts.

Some attribute the Evangelicals' success in Guatemala to their strong opposition to gambling, alcohol, and domestic violence, and their ability to provide a sense of order, identity, and belonging that counteracts the instability that people have felt for many years. The Protestant denominations have traditionally been less tolerant of syncretic practices than the Catholics, and some Evangelicals insist that indigenous deities like Maximón should be retired, viewing such syncretic beliefs and practices as satanic and growing out of witchcraft.

The Maya, many of whom retain strong beliefs in traditional practices, feel that Evangelical groups targeting their communities are a threat to their identity and culture, while the Catholic Church is generally more tolerant of Maya beliefs and customs.

FAMILY VALUES

A few generations ago, Guatemalan families were very large, with five to seven children being common. Nowadays, the average across the country is 2.4 children per couple, although families tend to be larger in Maya and rural communities and smaller in the larger cities, due to the financial pressures of city life. Households often include grandparents and the spouses or partners of children. Brothers, sisters, aunts, uncles, and cousins often live nearby and keep in regular contact, helping each other out when the need arises.

With families living together so closely and supporting each other, it's not surprising that the family is the most important unit in the life of Guatemalans. Respect for family, and especially elders, is instilled at a young age, and people spend a great deal of time with their extended family.

Rich or poor, grandparents and other elderly relatives typically remain in the family house to be cared for by younger relatives, rather than moving to an assisted-living facility or retirement community. Guatemalans who have lived abroad sometimes comment on the "coldness" of people in the US or UK, who tend to live in a nuclear family unit, spend less time with relatives, and are prepared to let others care for their elderly parents.

Children typically stay at home while they study at college or university, and fly the nest only after they marry. Men often wait to marry until they are in a financial position to start a home of their own, so thirty-something bachelors living with their parents are quite common. It's also typical to find single mothers living at the family home and relying on their parents to help bring up their children.

Even when it comes to vacations, it's typical for extended families to travel together and share the joy of a trip to the beach, a visit to a colonial city, or just a day trip into the highlands to eat a regional speciality.

There are also constant rounds of celebrations that

help to cement family bonds, such as birthdays, marriages, christenings, *quinceañeras* (the fifteenth-birthday parties for girls), Christmas and New Year festivities, and all the local indigenous festivals like the Festival de Barriletes Gigantes (Giant Kite Festival) in Sumpango during Todos Santos (All Saints Day, or Day of the Dead), and the Rabin Ajaw festival in Cobán, Alta Verapaz.

CARIÑO AND DIMINUTIVE ENDEARMENTS

Cariño, when used as a noun, means darling, love, or sweetie-pie, as in: "*Hola, cariño*" (Hi, honey). As a verb it means to show affection, love, or friendship with others, both physically and in speech, and it plays an integral part of communication in Guatemala. Locals demonstrate affection by greeting each other with a hug or a kiss on the cheek. It's also evident during conversations, such as when touching a person's shoulder or arm while talking, or standing closer to one's interlocutor than northern Europeans and Americans may be used to. Guatemalans from rural indigenous communities are generally more reserved than their urban counterparts, however.

Spanish is full of endearments, but in Guatemala you are more likely to hear people using the diminutive forms -ito and -ita, which are added to the end of a word to transform it into a smaller or sweeter version. So, *mi amor* (my love) becomes *mi amorcito* (my little love), *abuela* (grandmother) becomes *abuelita*, and *amigo* (friend) becomes a very friendly *amiguito*. Diminutives can also be used in an unfriendly way to put somebody down. *Hombrecito* (little man) is endearing when used to describe a child, but if a man in a face-off with another man uses the term it is intended to insult.

Guatemalans also love to give their family and friends an *apodo* (nickname). Some are affectionate, others more of a tease. If you have curly hair they might call you *colocho* (curly), or *colochito*. If you are fair-haired, you might hear *canche* (blondie). You will also hear people call each other *pelón* (baldy), *gordo* (fatty), *flaco* (skinny), or, if they have indigenous heritage, *Chinito* (Chinese-looking).

Some of these "endearments" do not always translate literally in a way that makes sense to outsiders. Context is everything. If the tone of voice is friendly and the words accompanied with a smile, you can rest assured that the name they've just called you is meant affectionately. Among a group of Guatemalan friends, a nickname is often a sign of acceptance.

GUATE TIME

For uptight Westerners tied to the clock, the concept of "Guate Time" can be a constant frustration. For Guatemalans who deal with considerably more challenging travel conditions and who live through earthquakes and hurricanes on a fairly regular basis, being a few minutes late is no big deal.

In general, punctuality is not a consideration, especially if something more important occurs. *Mañana* means "tomorrow," and indicates that time can be viewed flexibly. Rather than assuming that Guatemalans are irresponsible or slackers, it's important to remember that, for most of them, time consciousness is simply not a top priority. These ideas about time are also a product of the attitude that the quality of an interaction is more important than how long it lasts. It's fairly common for Guatemalans to arrive thirty minutes or more behind schedule for an appointment or meeting. For them, 4:00 p.m. can mean any time between 4:00 and 5:00 p.m.—what's important is showing up, and the quality of the time spent together.

DIVORCE AND ABORTION

Divorce is legal in Guatemala, despite long-standing opposition from the Catholic Church and conservative politicians, but the country's divorce rate is among the lowest in the world. In 2023, international surveys showed Guatemala's divorce rate was as low as one divorce for every five thousand people. (For comparison, in the US it is around fifteen per five thousand.) Some of the reasons for this include the traditional values promoted by the Catholic Church, the growing influence of evangelist Protestant churches that preach the sanctity of marriage, and the ancestral nature of indigenous belief that is grounded in the family unit and the home. Other prac-tical factors include the steps needed to get a divorce, the difficulties of securing spousal maintenance, and the fact that many families live on or below the poverty line and simply cannot afford to divorce.

In 2011, First Lady Sandra Torres filed for divorce

from her husband, President Alvaro Colom, so she could run for president herself and bypass constitutional laws banning close relatives of the president from running for the top office. She had already been divorced once and was Colom's third wife. She said she was "leaving a loving marriage for the sake of the nation." Things didn't quite work out as hoped in this case, however, as she was unsuccessful in her presidential campaigns of 2015, 2019, and 2023.

The Catholic Church's entrenched opposition to abortion means that it's still illegal, except in extreme cases where the life of the mother would be put in danger by giving birth. Sanctions are harsh, although seldom enforced, with a one-to-three-year prison sentence for a woman who has an abortion and a similar sentence for the person who carries it out. The law means many women, especially in rural areas where health clinics are rare, must endanger their lives to terminate a pregnancy by turning to backstreet abortionists.

RESPECT, *SIMPATÍA*, AND NONCONFRONTATION

In general, Guatemalans like to pursue smooth interpersonal relationships and avoid conflict and confrontation. Overall, they value indirectness, respect, and formality in interactions, particularly with people they may not be familiar with. Respect (*respeto*) is given to individuals of greater status or power, such as the elderly and wealthy people, and requires courteous and polite behavior. Typically, a person is much better received and more likely to have successful interactions when they demonstrate the appropriate respect. Guatemalans tend to be sensitive to the opinions of others and are extremely proud, so it's important not to humiliate or embarrass anyone in public, or somehow cause them to lose dignity. If there is direct confrontation, many Guatemalans are likely to be offended, and may go as far as ending the friendship.

Simpatía, a related value, technically translates as "sympathy," but the meaning of the word in Spanish has more to do with pleasantness and congeniality, with an emphasis on interpersonal harmony and easy relationships. In Guatemala, direct argument or conflict is considered rude. Confrontation is not valued and most Guatemalans will avoid it at all costs, preferring to acquiesce or to become overtly agreeable.

In part, this desire to avoid confrontation may stem from the army's reign of terror in Guatemala, when it was better to answer questions vaguely and according to whoever was doing the asking rather than answer directly. This can still be seen today, especially in rural areas. A tourist might ask for directions, and a typical response would be, "Oh, that way," or "Who knows?" whether the person knows the answer or not.

ATTITUDES TOWARD WOMEN IN A MACHO WORLD

As elsewhere in Latin America, gender inequality and machismo are deeply ingrained in society. Boys are still mollycoddled by their mothers and rarely asked to do domestic chores like cooking and cleaning, which are usually assigned to sisters and female relatives. Boys also have more freedom to roam outside the house. Men can more easily get away with having more than one girlfriend, or taking a mistress when married, as there is an expectation that "boys will be boys!", but they are also expected to provide for and protect the family.

Guatemalan women—especially mothers and grandmothers—are still the backbone of the family, and are expected to provide for children, manage household income, work, cook, and clean. Traditional attitudes are changing, especially in slightly more progressive places like Guatemala City and Antigua, and many more Guatemalan women from all over the country are studying, working outside the home, and pursuing careers.

The dark side of machismo is reflected in the prevalence of domestic violence, sexual assault, and the high incidence of femicides—the murders of Guatemalan women and girls, often by a partner. This culture of violence against women is perpetuated by machismo, but also by a weak justice system in which few crimes are solved and perpetrators feel they can act with impunity.

ATTITUDES TO FOREIGNERS

Foreign tourists bring income, which is of course desirable, and Guatemalans are genuinely curious and welcoming to tourists visiting their country. The Covid-19 pandemic caused great hardship in areas of the country dependent on tourism, and there was great relief to see visitor numbers bounce back.

However, there are unfortunate rumors in circulation

about tourists that some indigenous people believe to be true. These include stories about visitors stealing Maya babies, and also locals giving away children to tourists so they will have a better life. Many Guatemalans have the perception that all Westerners are rich. This view comes partly from the fact that tourists seem able to travel to Guatemala easily, some from long distances, meaning expensive plane tickets, whereas for many Guatemalans overseas travel is impossibly expensive. In addition, Guatemalans are constantly exposed to Western images of fashion and pop culture, which contributes to a belief that all people in the US and Europe lead similarly glamorous and luxurious lives.

Overall, despite the myths and false perceptions, foreigners can be expected to be greeted with warmth and hospitality, and will find people eager to promote the charms and natural beauty of their country.

ATTITUDES TO FOREIGN WOMEN

Guatemalan men are friendly and respectful to women in general, as they are to men. There are some cases where a foreign woman is seen as an opportunity to live abroad or a meal ticket, and for that reason women travelers should exercise sensible caution if faced with advances of a romantic nature. Women travel solo all over Guatemala, but it's wise to plan ahead, avoid rundown areas, heed local advice, and join other travelers or take a guide for trips off the beaten track.

For most women travelers, the macho attitudes and

lame pickup lines are annoying rather than threatening, especially sugary endearments in the street like *mi reina* (my queen), *mi corazon* (my heart), and *psst psst, mamacita!* to get your attention. The best approach is to do what the local Chapínas do: ignore it.

ATTITUDES TO THE MAYA

Guatemala makes much of its Maya heritage, both the magnificent ancient cities like Tikal and the weaving traditions of modern Maya communities for which the country is famous, but attitudes toward the Maya themselves are still shaped by the Spanish conquest and the subjugation of the indigenous people, a system of *encomiendas* that gave control over indigenous communities to Spanish overlords, in a system similar to Medieval serfdom in Europe.

The belief that Spanish or European culture was superior to indigenous culture became the norm. That belief was then shared by the newly created mestizo or Ladino population, with a hierarchy that started with Europeans at the top of the pyramid, Ladinos in the middle, and indigenous Maya and other groups at the bottom. The disrespectful term "Indio" (Indian) is still used by Ladinos and Maya to refer to indigenous people, despite its racist undertones. In terms of jobs, Maya workers are more likely to be employed in low-paid manual labor, or on farms as day laborers, or working from home to weave textiles or produce handicrafts. Many Maya women work as maids, nannies, cooks, or housekeepers for Ladino families.

That picture is changing, as the Maya and other indigenous groups take more control over the future of their communities, looking back to the achievements of their ancient ancestors, national heroes like the K'iche' Maya warrior king Tecun Uman, and the modern-day diversity of indigenous languages, colorful *trajes*, and full calendar of folk fiestas that has survived and thrived.

Pride in indigenous culture has seen the emergence of popular performing artists like the young Kaqchikel singer songwriter Sara Curruchich, who includes both Maya and Spanish in rousing songs that celebrate her indigenous roots and call for greater acceptance of Maya in society.

LGBTQ IN A MACHO SOCIETY

The strict teachings of the Catholic Church and the prevailing macho culture in the country mean that attitudes toward homosexuality and the LGBTQ community are not as progressive or as accepting in Guatemala as they are in countries like the US or Canada.

Homosexuality has been legal since 1871, but same-sex marriages or civil unions are not legally recognized, which limits the legal rights of same-sex partners living together.

In politics, the main political parties are socially conservative and are as opposed to progressive legislation on LGBTQ issues as they are to abortion. There are no specific laws against discrimination based on sexual orientation or gender identity. You can apply to a court to legally change your name if you are transgender but you cannot change your legal gender.

The political landscape has been slowly changing, especially with the election to Congress in 2015 of Sandra Morán, Guatemala's first openly homosexual politician. Morán organized Guatemala's first lesbian group in the 1990s.

There has been an annual Pride march in Guatemala City for many years, but it was nearly stopped in 2024 after a legal challenge by a conservative lawyer who objected to the LGBTQ procession on moral grounds. The Constitutional Court rejected the case but urged the organizers to keep in mind "the protection of spiritual and moral social values, especially in the case of children and teenagers."

Many LGBTQ people in Guatemala end up living *tapado* (in the closet) to avoid discrimination, a situation highlighted in the award-winning 2018 film *José*, directed by Li Cheng, that stars Guatemalan actor Enrique Salanic as a young nineteen-year-old who struggles to keep his sexuality a secret from his strictly Catholic mother.

LGBTQ visitors to Guatemala will find people welcoming and hospitable, but discretion is advised when it comes to public displays of affection. There is not much of an LGBTQ community in rural areas, but in Antigua and Guatemala City there is a well-established and vibrant gay scene. As tourism grows there is also an increasingly open attitude in the party towns of Panajachel and San Pedro in Lago de Atitlán, and the small surfing towns of the Pacific coast.

CHAPTER THREE

CUSTOMS & TRADITIONS

Religion in Guatemala has developed and blended over the centuries, and continues to remain an important part of both Maya and Ladino culture. Guatemala is officially a Catholic country and has been this way since colonization began over five centuries ago. However, many indigenous Maya have held on to their traditional spiritual beliefs, and in the highlands traditional priests can be found who practice the secret rituals and customs of the Maya.

THE MAYA AND CATHOLIC FESTIVALS

Traditional Maya religion as practiced by the warrior-priest rulers of the ancient Maya was not completely lost as a result of the Spanish conquest and the forced conversion of indigenous people carried out by the Catholic Church over centuries.

The survival of Maya culture is a remarkable tribute to the millions of Maya who resisted colonization and clung on to their languages, customs, *trajes*, and ancient cosmovision, often by worshiping the old gods in secret, or disguising their worship by expressing it under the guise of Catholic tradition and the worship of Catholic saints, a practice known as syncretism.

In many Maya villages there is a religious *cofradía* (brotherhood) of indigenous male elders who look after a particular saint in the village church and in their own small chapel or house until it's time for it to take its place in the fiesta for its Catholic feast day, when it's paraded through the streets. Being part of the *cofradía* is an honor that conveys respect on those who participate, but is also a financial burden, as they are expected to cover the costs of organizing the celebrations.

For those who follow ancient Maya traditions, native Aj'itz (literally "Day Lords" or "daykeepers"), often translated as shamans, are the intermediaries between ordinary mortals and the gods and spirits, and they are seen as the spiritual and cultural descendants of the ruling priestly elite of classic Maya civilization. They preside over rituals that take place in a mountain cave or at a sacred Maya site and involve prayers, invocations, the burning of copal resin and the offering of incense, alcohol, and sometimes animal blood to the gods.

Traditional Maya healing practices also include invocations, alcohol, the burning of copal incense, and offerings, and are carried out by a *curandero* (healer) or *zahorín*.

MAXIMÓN, THE MAYA SAINT

Under Spanish rule, Maya religion and rituals were prohibited; but people continued to practice their religion in private, which has led to a blending of Maya and Christian beliefs and rituals. In some cases, the Maya have taken Catholic saints and imbued them with the characteristics of ancient Maya deities.

One of the most interesting examples of a folk saint is Maximón, or Saint Simone, venerated in many Guatemalan villages. Maximón is a maize god, an anti-saint of sorts, who is known for his love of drinking and smoking.

According to legend, Maximón was supposed to take care of the women while the men were out working in the fields. His way of "taking care" of them was to sleep with them, thus enraging their husbands, who cut off his arms and legs in revenge.

Today, Maximón is represented by a dummy figure who is dressed and cared for in various chapels or worshipers' homes. Locals come to ask for his help with problems caused by misdemeanors (such as that of a relative in jail, or an alcoholic uncle), bringing gifts of *aguardiente* (schnapps) and cigars to appeal to him. Many Maya believe that he can protect them from evil spirits, and help them in their quest for wives, jobs, and riches.

ATTITUDE TO RELIGION

Religion plays a key role in Guatemala. Catholicism came
to present-day Guatemala with the Spanish conquest
of 1524, and established itself immediately with the
construction of the squat Church of San Jacinto in
Salcajá, the oldest Catholic church in Central America.
Franciscans and other missionaries built churches,
chapels, and convents, and set about the wholesale
conversion of the indigenous population. To root out
and destroy "heretical" Maya worship, bark books of
hieroglyphic symbols, known as codices, were burnt
on bonfires, and the inquisition sought out heretics to
punish. Forced to practice their rituals in secret, the
Maya adapted Catholic saints and Church feast days
to their Maya belief system, creating a syncretic fusion
that continues today.

Today, some 45 percent of the population are
estimated to be Catholic and around 40 percent are
estimated to be Protestant, mainly Evangelical. Worship
takes many forms, from traditional Catholic services to
outdoor revivals and informal preaching on the chicken
buses. Typically, evangelical services include singing and
sometimes dancing. Most revivals, which usually occur
on Saturday evenings, have a loud amplified band that
accompanies the singing.

Among the Maya there is no one unified religion,
although there are deities that hark back to ancient times
that are invoked in prayers, and a cosmovision that sees
mountains, trees, and caves as imbued with a spirit. Some
Maya are Catholic, some are Evangelical Protestants,
and others are traditional, practicing their Maya belief

system in a number of different ways. It's very common to see ancient Maya rituals being performed by an *aj'itz* at ancient Maya ruins, cemeteries, and caves throughout the country. Sometimes they involve animal sacrifices, from which tourists are usually excluded.

Other religions in Guatemala include the Church of Jesus Christ of Latter-day Saints (Mormons), Jehovah's Witnesses, Judaism, Islam, and followers of the Indian spiritual leader Sri Sathya Sai Baba. The Mennonites also have a following in Guatemala, and are recognized by their distinctive minimalist appearance and way of life, including their famous baked goods and dairy products.

FESTIVALS AND HOLIDAYS

Guatemala's indigenous *fiestas* are some of the most distinctive in Latin America and follow the Catholic calendar of religious celebrations that mark moveable feast days like Semana Santa (Holy Week/Easter), Corpus Christi, and Carnaval, while preserving ancient Maya beliefs and customs. They generally include processions, costumes, and traditional masks, and can be very noisy, with loud firecrackers and merrymaking along with heavy alcohol consumption and special dishes. Each town and village has at least one day a year that is devoted to celebrating the local saint, with some areas extending the party by a week or two around the special day. In predominantly Ladino areas, most fiestas have religious processions (in which the patron saint is carried through the streets), as well as beauty contests (with contestants riding on the backs of cars, trucks, or horses), marching bands and majorettes, street food stalls, and marimba or cumbia concerts that go on through the night.

PUBLIC HOLIDAYS

Government offices and businesses like banks and large stores tend to shut down completely on public holidays, which can be frustrating for tourists on a tight schedule. When a public holiday falls on a Thursday or a Tuesday, many people will take the Friday or the Monday as an extra day off—known as a *puente* (bridge)—so that they can enjoy a four-day weekend.

January 1 New Year's Day

March/April Semana Santa (Holy Week): Jueves Santo (Maundy Thursday), Viernes Santo (Good Friday), and Domingo de Resurrección (Easter Sunday)

May 1 Labor Day

June 30 Army Day (anniversary of the 1871 Revolution)

August 15 Día de la Virgen de la Asunción (only in Guatemala City)

September 15 Independence Day

October 12 Día de la Raza or Día de la Resistencia Indígena (only banks are closed)

October 20 Revolution Day

November 1 All Saints' Day

December 24 Christmas Eve (from midday)

December 25 Christmas Day

December 31 (from noon) New Year's Eve

Año Viejo (December 31)

Like many people around the world, Guatemalans like to greet Año Nuevo (New Year) with a big meal and a party. Families gather together at home to enjoy a large meal, which is eaten late, between 9:00 p.m. and midnight. Turkey is gaining popularity as a festive food, but traditionally Guatemalans will prepare the same foods as they eat for Christmas dinner: roast suckling pig or turkey, *tamales colorados*, and *rompope* (eggnog). New Year's Eve parties are generally lively events, with dancing to festive music such as cumbias, reggaeton, and the Latin pop hits of the day.

Many Guatemalans will dress up in *estrenos* (new clothes) so that they start the year looking good. Some Guatemalan women believe that wearing red underwear on New Year's Eve will bring them love, yellow underwear money. Some people put Q100 in their right pocket to bring prosperity. A popular tradition is to try to eat twelve grapes on the twelve strokes of midnight to bring luck in the following twelve months; another is to sweep out the house. Some people write out a list of bad things that have happened over the past year and burn it, so they start the year fresh.

Semana Santa (March/April)

In this strongly Catholic country, Semana Santa (Holy Week) brings a week of religious ceremonies and special masses commemorating the crucifixion and resurrection of Jesus Christ, with processions of wooden statues paraded through the streets by hooded penitents, often accompanied with the music of brass bands and the creation of sawdust *alfombras* (carpets). Leading up to Semana Santa is La Cuaresma (Lent), forty days during which Catholics

Participants at Domingo de Palma (Palm Sunday) celebrations.

traditionally abstain from meat. On Fridays during Lent, communities across Guatemala reenact the Via Crucis (the Stations of the Cross), with some devotees dressed as Roman soldiers, while others drag heavy wooden crosses as an act of penitence and expression of faith to remember Christ's sufferings during the crucifixion.

The most colorful tradition takes place in Antigua, where the famous *alfombras* made of colored sawdust create images telling the story of the Passion of Christ. Domingo de Palma (Palm Sunday) marks the official start of Semana Santa, with the faithful carrying palm

fronds. Viernes Santo (Good Friday) is also a day
for reenactments of the Stations of the Cross. Easter
concludes with Domingo de Resurrección (Easter
Sunday), a joyous celebration of the resurrection, when
statues of Jesus and the Virgin Mary are traditionally
brought together.

Palo Volador in Cubulco, Baja Verapaz (July 25)

In a surviving expression of Maya ceremony, the
villagers of Cubulco erect a thirty-three-foot (ten-meter)
palo (tree trunk) in front of the whitewashed colonial
church to celebrate Saint John the Apostle's annual
feast day. Men wearing masks representing Spanish-
looking *Moros* (Moors) and *monos* (monkeys) perform
a traditional dance, before the *voladores* (flyers) ascend
the palo and swing on ropes hooked to their feet that
fly them slowly down to the ground.

Rabin Ajau (End of July)

A Maya beauty contest with a difference, the annual
Rabin Ajau festival is celebrated in the city of Cobán,
Alta Verapaz, on the last Saturday of July with street
parades, dancing, and fireworks. Started in 1969 as a
way to empower Maya women, the name of the festival
translates as "Daughter of the King." Competitors from
all over Guatemala are judged on their language skills,
knowledge of Maya traditions, and ability to talk
about issues that affect women in their communities.
The winner is awarded a silver crown adorned with
quetzal feathers.

INDIGENOUS RESISTANCE REPLACES COLUMBUS DAY

Celebrating Columbus Day on October 12, to mark the day in 1492 that Christopher Columbus is said to have arrived in the Americas, is no longer considered politically correct in most countries of Latin America, given the subsequent conquest, forced conversion, and cruel treatment meted out to indigenous Americans by the Spanish conquistadors, and the deaths of countless others from the European diseases they brought to the Americas. This has led many in Guatemala to adopt the term "Día de la Resistencia Indígena" (Indigenous Resistance Day), with less emphasis on Columbus and a greater focus on events that celebrate indigenous groups and the survival of their culture, history, and traditions.

Todos Santos (November 1)

Starting October 31, Todos Santos (Day of the Dead) is when Guatemalans remember the loved ones they have lost by visiting cemeteries to clean their graves, touch up tombs with fresh paint, and bring their favorite food and drink to share with them. Typical is *fiambre*, a sumptuous sharing dish unique to Guatemala with up to fifty ingredients that can include cold and cured meats, boiled eggs, sweet corn, onions, beets, pickled vegetables, cheese, and a salad dressing. Each family has their own recipe. Family altars and graves are also adorned with fresh *flores*

Families and friends in Santiago Sacatepequez prepare to launch giant colorful kites bearing traditional Maya motifs to honor the dead.

de muerto (marigold) flowers, which are believed to lead the deceased to the offerings laid out for them.

Other Todos Santos traditions include the colorful Festival de Barriletes Grandes (The Festival of Giant Kites) in Sumpango; the drunken horse racing through the narrow streets of Todos Santos Cuchumatán; and the three Santas Calaveras (Holy Skulls) in San José, a village on the north shore of Lago Petén Itzá, that are brought out from the Catholic church, blessed by a Catholic priest, and paraded around town.

Drunken horse racing to celebrate Todos Santos in the town of Todos Santos Cuchumatá.

Garífuna Settlement Day (November 26)

The biggest party on Guatemala's Caribbean coast, tiny Livingston throbs to the beat of Garífuna drums, maracas, and conch trumpets for three days to mark Garífuna Settlement Day. Celebrations start in earnest with a reenactment of the first settlers arriving in Livingston on rustic rafts decorated with the Garífuna flag, followed by street parades through the streets of town. As night falls the dancing intensifies as *punta* rock bands take to the stage and the *gifity* moonshine starts to flow.

Quema del Diablo (December 7)

Considered the start of Christmas festivities, the Quema del Diablo (Burning of the Devil) takes place on December 7 and involves burning large papier mâché effigies of red devils and setting off fireworks. It is considered a spiritual cleansing before December 8, which celebrates the immaculate conception of the Virgin Mary.

Breakfast With a Bang—Guatemalans Love Firecrackers!

Don't be alarmed if you are woken up by what sounds like gunshots as early as 5:00 in the morning. Guatemalans use firecrackers (*cuetes*) to celebrate anything and everything! Expect to hear early morning firecrackers for birthdays, holidays, anniversaries, and really anything else worth celebrating. December seems to be an especially fervent firecracker month, with the morning blast occurring almost every day.

Festive firecrackers being let off in Chichicastenango.

CHAPTER FOUR

MAKING FRIENDS

Guatemalans are very sociable, and start building the majority of their friendships at a young age. Extended family members provide key relationships and it's common for extended families to get together frequently, maybe two or three times a month, to eat, drink, enjoy the party, and catch up on the latest news.

For foreigners, it's easy to meet Guatemalans at Spanish schools, at work, or on nights out at bars and clubs. You can expect them to be very friendly, but it may be harder for you to form deep, long-lasting friendships. It takes time to build trust, and trust is at the heart of relationships for Guatemalans.

Generally, close friends in Guatemala have known each other for many years. It's also fairly common to see cousins, aunts, nephews, and cousins socializing or living together in extended family groups.

As in many relationship-based societies, people often ask favors of their friends, and expect them to grant them. The underlying principle seems to be,

"You scratch my back, and I'll scratch yours." By the same token, foreigners can expect their Guatemalan friends to help them out in different ways, such as accompanying them while they travel, providing assistance with running errands, health needs, gift purchases, and so on.

Guatemalans may refer to foreigners in a joking way as "*gringos*," but this is not meant in a derogatory way. They refer to themselves as Guatemaltecos or more informally as Chapínes. Some young people wear baseball hats and T-shirts with the slogan "100 Percent Chapín."

MAKING FRIENDS WITH GUATEMALANS

Visitors to Guatemala, both short- and long-term, find it easy to strike up friendships with the locals they meet. Guatemalans love to hang out and share a good-natured laugh and a joke, although deeper friendships, as anywhere in the world, take longer to form.

Most Guatemalans have a social circle that centers principally on the family and then extends to neighbors, school friends, and coworkers. Friends may be invited home for a special event such as a birthday party, christening, or wedding, but generally friends meet up away from the house. Foreigners working in Guatemala can expect to be invited by coworkers to join them for an after-work drink or a meal out, which is a good first step toward making friends. If you turn the offer down, you might be thought standoffish.

An invitation home to meet the family is a significant compliment. Make sure to take a gift—perhaps something from your country, or beer or rum if you know that your hosts drink. Whatever the setting, bear in mind that all attempts you make to speak Spanish, eat traditional dishes, join in the dancing, and generally have fun will be greatly appreciated. Failure to join in will see you labeled an *aguafiestas* (a killjoy, or party pooper).

Because some Guatemalans have the perception that all Western tourists are wealthy, and they themselves have high levels of poverty, it's not uncommon for a Westerner to be asked for money or other help by a well-intentioned Guatemalan friend. Some Maya Guatemalans view foreigners with suspicion and, as we have seen, there are a number of myths about Westerners and their behavior that can influence interactions. However, a persistent effort on your part will turn suspicion to trust and friendship.

Do What the Guatemalans Do

Guatemalans are friendly and sociable, but they are also very respectful of visitors to their country. If you don't speak to them, only give one word answers to their questions, or stick like glue to your traveling companions, they will assume you are not interested in making friends. This is especially true with the Maya, who are generally more reserved than Ladinos.

To break the ice you need to be proactive, make eye contact, smile, and use the Spanish or Maya words you know. Just as the locals do, make a point of saying "*Buenos días!*" (Good day), "*Buenas tardes!*" (Good afternoon), or just "*Buenas!*" when you walk into a room or meet people in the street.

Get used to saying *Hola!* (Hi) to the people you meet in a lift or sitting next to you on the chicken bus. Introduce yourself with a simple phrase like "*Mi nombre*

es…" (My name is…), then ask people for their names
with "*Y tu?*" (And you?).

As your confidence improves, throw in some Guate-
speak to show your appreciation, such as "*Chilero!*"
(Cool! Amazing!). (For more on local words and phrases,
see Chapter 9.)

EXPAT GROUPS

For expats living in Guatemala who want to socialize
with other foreign nationals and swap experiences, there
is a growing community of expats who live, work, or are
enjoying their retirement in Guatemala, especially in
Guatemala City, colonial Antigua, and the colorful
towns around Lago de Atitlan.

These expat communities are swollen in the winter
months by "snowbirds" from the US and Canada who
come for the vibrant culture, Maya ruins, indigenous
textiles, temperate climate, proximity to home, and
affordable cost of living. There is also an ever-growing
number of foreign nationals taking advantage of an
extended stay to study Spanish.

The international social networking group InterNations
has a chapter in Guatemala City that offers young and
not-so-young expats the opportunity to meet up with
old hands and locals at cocktail evenings, game nights,
sporty socials, and day-trip outings.

There are also a number of expat groups on Facebook
focused on specific cities in Guatemala, such as
Guatemala City and Antigua, where you can turn for
advice on everything from where to find your favorite

Young couple in downtown Guatemala City.

brand of peanut butter or satisfy a hankering for sushi to how to fill out visa extension forms.

THE DATING GAME

"Buscando amor" (looking for love) is hard enough at home, without all the cultural nuances involved in being in a new country with a different culture and language, so don't expect an easy ride as a newcomer. Women generally start having families quite young in Guatemala, people live at home until they get married, and the dating game is still quite traditional. For many rural couples, a date might consist of sitting on a bench in the Plaza Central, holding hands, and sharing a *granizada* (shaved ice).

Just as in dancing, when it comes to love men are expected to lead. The positive side of this old-school approach is manifested in the general courtesies and gallantry shown to women. A man is expected to open doors for a woman, pay for everything on a night out, and make sure she is delivered safely to her door. A woman can expect to receive flowery declarations and effusive compliments (*piropos*).

A less positive aspect is the possessiveness and jealousy that a macho culture can foster. There is also the fear that expressions of romance are more about finding a better future than true heartfelt emotions.

In big towns and cities, younger Guatemalans are increasingly looking for love via their smartphones, on apps like Tinder. Dating websites can also be a useful way to meet people, but steer clear of the ones that specifically want to match local women with foreign men, as they tend to be less about love and more about money. The best way to *ligar* (hook up) in Guatemala is probably to follow the same advice for finding friends: go out and meet people in the real world.

Guatemalans are happy to play matchmaker, and if you build up a group of local friends—especially at a language school, volunteering project, or workplace— they will soon start introducing you to possible soulmates.

Guatemalans like going out in groups, and might insist on bringing a cousin or friend along on a first date to take the pressure off. If you don't find romance on a date, at least you've expanded your social circle.

HOSPITALITY

As a people, Guatemalans are hospitable, polite, and accommodating, and tourists are generally appreciated as adding to the economy. Guatemalans like to give a good impression and will do so at all costs, even if it means

Pass the *pollo*: family dinner in Quetzaltenango.

hiding the reality of a harsh life. In Maya communities, visitors may at first be treated rather distantly, but upon getting to know people and building up relationships, they can expect to be treated with warmth.

It's common to be invited to a Guatemalan home for lunch, the biggest meal of the day. This generally involves a large spread of food and lively conversation. Expect to be offered second and third helpings by the hostess, a common method of welcoming a visitor into the home.

GIFT GIVING

In Guatemala the giving of gifts is one of the ways people maintain good interpersonal relationships. For example, if you are visiting someone's home for dinner, it's important to bring something small, such as a bunch of flowers or a bottle of good rum or wine, depending on what your hosts drink. Avoid flowers specifically used for funerals (which are generally white). If you are invited for lunch, you could bring a dessert. (See more on gift giving in Chapter 8.)

CONVERSATION STARTERS AND STOPPERS

Guatemalans come from large extended families, live much of their lives out on the street, and are highly sociable. When it gets too hot they might relax in front of the house, shooting the breeze with their neighbors, or sit in the local plaza hanging out with friends and neighbors. They like to socialize in groups and keep conversations light, focusing on things they have in common.

When you meet Guatemalans you can expect questions about your family, your country, how many hours it took you to get to Guatemala by plane, and your favorite music, food, beer, and football team.

You will also be asked what you think about Guatemala. Considering how proud people are of their country, and how hard they have fought in the past to battle dictators, natural disasters, low wages, and high unemployment, launching into a critique of the country will not be well received. The locals might gripe about the gridlocked traffic in Guatemala City, the corruption in local politics, or the problems of finding work, but they won't appreciate a foreign visitor doing the same. Another topic to gently sidestep is religion. Catholicism is the accepted religion, but Protestant denominations will defend their faith if they feel it is being criticized, and the indigenous Maya are very proud and protective of their belief system. It's a question of respect.

You will raise a smile by coming up with a local phrase like *Es chilero!* (It's cool!) when describing your favorite local dish, a beautiful part of the country you have visited, or the friendliness of the people you have met on your travels.

Whatever the topic of conversation, approach it with curiosity, but also a sense of humor and a willingness to learn.

LEARNING SPANISH

Guatemala is one of the most popular and economical countries for foreigners who want to study Spanish, and there are plenty of schools that have made this into a big industry. Some of the schools are well established, while some are relatively new, and may hold classes in the front room of someone's home. Antigua and Quetzaltenango are the two most popular cities for students, with numerous Spanish schools in each. Antigua has more tourists, while Quetzaltenango has fewer tourists and just as many schools. Many of these Spanish language schools provide homestays with native Guatemalans, and offer field visits and adventure trips with guides. It will also introduce you to a network of people—both local and foreign—in the same town that could form a basis for new friendships and people to explore the country with. If you don't already speak Spanish and have time when visiting, enrolling in a short Spanish course is something well worth considering.

CHAPTER FIVE

AT HOME

HOUSING

Houses in Guatemala are as varied as the people who live in them. What they look like depends on social class, whether the inhabitants are Ladino or Maya, and whether they are located in a rural or an urban area. Because the majority of Guatemalans live in some poverty, you will see a number of Ladino families living in what once was a beautiful colonial house that has become run-down over the years. Such houses in Guatemala typically feature an open central courtyard, with a living room, dining room, and bedrooms connected.

The majority of urban middle-class Ladinos, particularly outside the capital, are not wealthy. As such, their homes tend to be inadequately built, run-down, and sometimes structurally unstable. Then there are the shantytowns of tin-roofed shacks attached to the cities, where displaced Maya and impoverished Ladinos live.

There is, however, a small percentage of Ladinos living

in very nice colonial and Western-style homes, usually in the urban centers. There are also luxurious vacation homes, often owned by foreigners, available in tourist areas like Antigua and around Lake Atitlán.

Rural life is quite different. Most of the houses are built of adobe (sun-dried bricks) or breeze blocks, with thatched or zinc roofs. Some have one room or are partitioned, with a covered cooking area and a hearth out the back. Many houses lack indoor plumbing and will have a "washing area" for laundry, dishwashing, and bathing. Other houses lack this area altogether, and residents do their washing at the local river.

Electricity reaches almost everyone, except in the most remote areas, and is used primarily for light, refrigeration, TV, and of course the charging of cell phones.

FAMILY LIFE

Daily life revolves around the family in Guatemala. As we have seen, there is strong loyalty within families, even for extended family members, and it's common to see large families living in the same household. Guatemalans are not likely to spend much "alone time" as they are constantly socializing with family, extended family members, and friends.

Godparents (*padrinos*) are an important part of the family. Families are very tight-knit and children continue to rely on their parents for advice and guidance throughout their lives.

Traditionally, Ladino families have been medium to large in size, perhaps with four to six children living

A family in Guazacapan.

within a household, and possibly extra children of relatives or an ailing grandparent. Today, families are much smaller, as both partners have to work and two children is the norm.

Within Maya culture, families are usually large and life is extremely traditional. Men wield authority in Maya villages, while women are expected to run the home. Daily life revolves around the men tending the cornfields (*milpas*) and vegetable gardens while the women stay at home cooking, weaving, and looking after the children. Maya women travel with children in tow to out-of-town markets to sell handicrafts, textiles, and vegetables and fruits, as well as to trade for needed supplies.

Many Maya women serve as *domesticas* (housekeepers) for Ladino families, even if the Ladino family is not wealthy. Some *domesticas* are provided with room and board for the week and may travel back to their villages on the weekends. These women cook and clean, and sometimes look after their employers' children.

Traditional Guatemalan families are hierarchical, with the father as head of the household and special respect shown to the elderly grandparents. Mothers are expected to be self-sacrificing and obedient. Domestic violence is common in Guatemala but there are a number of educational campaigns aimed at challenging macho culture and encouraging victims to seek help.

For many women whose partner has been working abroad for many years, it can be especially tough to get by, and extended family ties play a strong part in helping them with childminding and sharing chores.

CHILDREN

Children are very important to Guatemalans—a household without children is thought to be lonely and sad. Guatemalan children are generally raised strictly and are expected to be obedient; but they are indulged when small, so they don't cry or complain too much.

Generally, Maya children are expected to contribute financially to the family as soon as they are capable. A very common sight in Guatemala is a young Maya woman carrying her baby on her back with a rectangular piece of material called a *tzute*. The baby stays on the mother's back while she works. Although legislation is in place to prohibit children from working, it's not unusual to see Maya children as young as five or six years old selling handicrafts to make money for the family. Ladino children are usually not expected to work until they are teenagers.

Boys tend to be afforded greater freedoms, while girls are often quite restricted. Older children are expected to take care of younger siblings, especially older sisters.

Many Guatemalan children of Maya origin are given away for international adoption because their mothers cannot support them due to extreme poverty, and because many young women have children out of wedlock, which is generally viewed as unacceptable.

There is also a large of "street children," (estimates are vague, but in the range of five thousand to ten thousand), mostly Maya, living in Guatemala City and other cities. These children are either runaways or castaways from families too poor to feed them. The majority are homeless, and sleep on a piece of cardboard on the sidewalks at night. During the daytime, they beg for money, scrounge food, and scavenge from dumpsters. They often spend hours high from sniffing glue or other inhalants, which are cheaper than most food. Many Ladino Guatemalans view the street children as a nuisance and worry only about the poor impression they make on tourists. There are very few shelters or organizations to help the children.

EDUCATION

Education is highly valued by most Guatemalans and is seen as a route to better employment. In Guatemala City, there are many private schools and colleges catering to

Students using the computer lab at their college in Guazacapan.

elite and middle-class Guatemalans, and a wide range of private language schools teaching English.

The public education system is compulsory and free to all children aged seven to sixteen, but is generally underfunded, suffers from staff shortages due to low pay, and does not cover the costs of uniforms, school supplies, or transport for low-income students.

There are six grades of primary (*primaria*) school, covering the ages seven to twelve. Despite being compulsory, attendance rates are low (about 75 percent) as enforcement is slack.

Secondary (*secundaria*) school is from ages twelve or thirteen to sixteen, when students receive a *Diploma de Estudios*. Those with good grades who want to continue in education to eighteen take an exam for the Bachillerato de Ciencias y Letras, which is needed to enter university. A three-year technical education program leading to the Perito Comercial, Industrial, Agricola, Técnico diploma is also available at the secondary level.

Higher education in Guatemala is provided by one public university (the Universidad de San Carlos de Guatemala) and some sixteen private universities. Instruction is in Spanish. The first-level degree at university is the Técnico or Diplomado, and is typically awarded after two to three and a half years of study. The next level is Licenciatura, which is awarded after four to five years of study and submission of a thesis (medicine requires six years). The third stage is the Maestría and Doctorado. The Maestría degree is given after one to two years of further study after the thesis, and the Doctorado is awarded after two consecutive years of study following the Licenciatura degree and thesis submission in Law, Humanities, Education, Economics, and Social Sciences.

While the public school system in Guatemala has its challenges, great strides have been made in recent years to improve reading and writing skills. The literacy rate among adults (Guatemalans aged fifteen and above) was above 80 percent in 2024, with adult males at 88 percent and adult females at 80 percent, according to figures from the World Bank.

However, among younger Guatemalans, those aged 15 to 24, the literacy rate is much higher, at 96 percent for both males and females.

EDUCATIONAL INEQUALITY

In education, as in other areas of Guatemalan society, there is a large gulf between the opportunities open to wealthy Guatemalan families and those living in cities, and the mainly indigenous Guatemalans living on much smaller incomes in rural or remote communities. One factor is the lack of schools, another the costs of uniforms, school supplies, and transport.

For some families who continue to subsist from traditional milpa agricultural practices, children who reach a certain age are expected to help out at home and in the fields. This particularly affects indigenous girls, many of whom drop out after primary school to care for siblings, weave textiles for sale, or assist their mothers at markets.

Some Maya believe formal school education is focused only on a Westernized Spanish-speaking curriculum that doesn't teach about their heritage and culture, although this is changing as more primary schools in indigenous areas now incorporate Maya language education as part of the school day.

This comes after decades of campaigning by the Academia de Lenguas Mayas (the Guatemalan Academy of Mayan Languages), which was established to revitalize Maya cultures and languages. The academy

standardized the Mayan alphabet so it could
more easily be taught in schools.

For Maya children whose families want them
to progress beyond the basic education available
in the villages, there are either public schools or
the more popular Catholic schools.

LEARNING ENGLISH

Given the rapid growth of English-speaking call center
jobs in Guatemala, it's no surprise that there are many
eager students who want to take English classes in
Guatemala's numerous private language schools. What
is a little more surprising is that so few Guatemalans are
conversational in English but rather only know a few
common terms, considering the compulsory English
classes children attend at primary and secondary
school, and the fact that so many families have relatives
living in the US. In tourist towns and major cities it's
not too hard to find somebody with some command
of English, but this is less likely in rural areas and even
rarer in indigenous communities, where even Spanish
is a second language.

One advantage of this keen interest in learning
English is that many people will want to practice their
English-language skills on you, and will hopefully
reciprocate by teaching you a few words or phrases
in Spanish.

Busting open a *piñata* at a children's birthday party, Guazacapan.

CYCLE OF FAMILY LIFE AND RITES OF PASSAGE

For both rich and poor the rituals that mark the cycle of life—births, baptisms, weddings, birthdays, and *quinceañera* parties—bring family and friends together. If you spend any time traveling in Guatemala, or have a job working alongside Guatemalans, you might well receive an invitation to one of these events. If you do, accepting the invitation will provide you with invaluable insight into Guatemalan life.

Milestones Marked by the Catholic Church

El bautizo (baptism), when a child receives his or her Christian name, is usually celebrated shortly after birth at a church service attended by family and close friends. This is a joyous occasion where gifts are given, and there is typically a post-baptism party with music, food, and drink.

Primera Comunión (First Communion) is when

young Catholics between the ages of seven and twelve first take the consecrated wafer and wine that symbolize the body and blood of Christ. Typically celebrated in a group, boys and girls dress all in white, with white gloves and a white candle symbolizing purity. Boys often wear long-sleeved *guayabera* shirts and girls wear veils or floral headbands.

Confirmación (Confirmation) takes place at around fifteen or sixteen years old, when young adults confirm their Catholic faith in the church at a special mass.

Sweet Fifteen
A major event for young Guatemalan girls is the Fiesta de Quince Años (Fifteenth Birthday Party), which is seen as a rite of passage. The elaborate celebrations more closely resemble that of a wedding than a Sweet Sixteen party in the US. Depending on the budget, the *quinceañera* dresses up in a ball gown with a crown or tiara, and is joined by her godparents and her closest friends who will also wear formal suits and dresses. Traditionally, a *quince* starts with Mass in church; then there are photographs on the church steps; and afterwards there's the party. The *quinceañera* dances a waltz with her father, followed by a toast, perhaps a serenade by a mariachi band, and then a live band or DJ who will play into the night.

Quinceañera presents can be extravagant. In the recent past, a trip to the US was all the rage for the daughters of the rich; nowadays presents can include tours around Europe, a car, even cosmetic surgery.

For poorer families the dress might be homemade, and the party held at home, but everybody tries to make the day special for the *quinceañera*.

LOVE AND MARRIAGE

In Guatemala the conduct of courtship is still quite
conservative, at least publicly, and reflects the continuation
of traditional Catholic values among Ladinos. Also
following age-old traditions, in some rural indigenous
communities respected family elders or godparents still
act as matchmakers for young couples, and the groom's
family is expected to pay the bride's parents a dowry.

Dating is important for young Guatemalans, and
couples tend to meet in public parks or at the central
square as there are limited places they can spend time
together alone. It isn't unusual to see teenage couples on
park benches, holding hands and stealing a kiss or two.

Many couples first meet through mutual friends or
at school or work, and being asked on a first date—just
like with marriage proposals—is usually down to the
man, although in the bigger cities dating apps are slowly
changing this as both men and women get to swipe right.

For young couples, marriage can often be brought about
by pregnancy, and women in general tend to marry young,
typically in their late teens. Sex education is not common
in Guatemala, and many parents avoid the topic with
their children.

Weddings tend to be large and joyful, with many
extended family members, including children and friends,
in attendance. There are flowers, dancing, and singing. In a
traditional Guatemalan wedding, the bride and groom may
choose to be tied together by a silver rope as a symbol of
their eternal bond. With Western-style church marriages
the bride wears white, while in indigenous communities
a more elegant version of *traje* provided to the bride by

the groom's family shows respect for traditions.

Most Ladino weddings follow a Catholic ceremony, but many also include traditional, non-Catholic elements. The bride and groom's godmothers often play an important role, offering their blessings. At Guatemalan weddings, it's common to see bell-shaped piñatas filled with raw beans, rice, and confetti.

Divorce is legal but Guatemala has one of the lowest divorce rates in the world, partly due to conservative Catholic ideals of marriage for life, but also because it can be complicated and expensive to get a divorce if either of the parties doesn't agree to it.

Many couples live together in a legally recognized *unión de hecho* (de facto union), which offers women more security under the law when it comes to housing and child custody if there is a separation.

Parents often support their children financially until they are married, and some newlyweds remain living with one set of parents for several years, often until they have children of their own.

DAILY LIFE

There are extreme contrasts in the standard and conduct of everyday life in Guatemala. Wealthy families who live in Guatemala City enjoy a cosmopolitan lifestyle similar to that in a European city. The daily life of the poor rural Maya remains very traditional, with the majority working in agriculture as subsistence farmers or day laborers, or in the production of handicrafts.

Morning routines for the majority of Guatemalans, whether Ladino or Maya, start early. In a typical Guatemalan family, the woman will wake at about 5:00 a.m. to begin household tasks such as washing clothes and preparing food. At around 6:00 a.m. she will wake her husband and school-age children and serve them breakfast. At 7:00 a.m., the father goes to work and the children to school. If the family has a *domestica* then she will go to the market, clean the house, and prepare lunch; otherwise the mother will do this work. At 1:00 p.m. school is over and most children come home for a big lunch. The remainder of the day is spent with the children, doing homework and extracurricular activities, or supplemental classes such as English, arts, sports, music, and math. Many families are heavy television watchers in the afternoon and evening, though as most families will only have one set in the house, it's not an entirely antisocial activity. Most children go to bed at 9:00 p.m. and the parents at around 10:30 to 11:00 p.m.

In rural areas, life revolves around agriculture, and the daily routine depends on the climate of the region. For example, in the coastal areas the men will wake up as early as 4:30 a.m. to begin work at 5:00 a.m. before it becomes too hot. The women mainly stay at home to care for the children and cook for the family; however, they will also do heavy labor when needed, such as climbing the mountains to cut and carry wood for the fires, washing clothes in the river, and carrying water for cooking and drinking. In rural areas, women accompanied by their children usually take lunch to the men working in the fields, and the family eats as a group.

MEALS

A typical breakfast consists of mashed or refried black beans, tortillas, fried or scrambled eggs with tomato, onion, ham or sausage, and plantains. It's usually eaten between 6:00 and 7:00 a.m. In rural areas, families may have *atol* (a corn- or rice-based drink) for breakfast. For very poor Guatemalans, the basic diet consists of corn, beans, and fruit.

Lunch is the main meal of the day, and is eaten sometime between 12 noon and 2:00 p.m. It usually consists of soup, tortillas, meat, and several side dishes of vegetables and fruits.

Supper is generally a more modest meal, and may simply consist of leftovers from lunch. In the larger cities, people may go out to eat, typically between 7:00 and 8:30 p.m., and have a more substantial dinner.

At every meal, before eating—during eating if someone interrupts—and after everyone has finished eating, Guatemalans always wish each other "*Buen provecho!*" which roughly means, "Good health!"

SHOPPING

Most Guatemalans in Guatemala City still frequent local markets, despite the widespread availability of modern supermarkets like the Walmart-owned Maxi Despensa and Despensa Familiar stores that stock everything you could imagine under one roof (and offer online shopping for delivery).

The biggest market in Guatemala is in San Francisco

el Alto on Fridays. Here anything and everything you want can be purchased, including food, clothing, and even livestock. Other famous markets include the Thursday and Sunday ones in Chichicastenango and the Friday market in Sololá. Almost every village has its weekly market day, when people come to trade their surplus produce and to socialize. On market days the plaza is full of activity, with people arriving in pickup trucks, on buses, by foot, and by donkey. Haggling is the name of the game. This is good-humored and does not usually involve raised voices, unless there is a mishap (which generally seems to involve foreigners, with the foreigners doing most of the yelling).

There are large supermarkets in the cities, and if a family has easy access to transportation, such as their own car or a minibus, it's quite likely that they will also shop here for food and housewares.

DRESS

In Guatemala City, other large cities, and popular tourist sites such as Antigua and Panajachel, a more Westernized and casual style of dress is common, with styles influenced by the US and Mexico, including baseball hats in towns and cowboy hats in rural or ranching areas.

For the Maya and other indigenous groups, most local women will proudly wear traditional clothing (*traje tipico*), which identifies their indigenous language community or their village. Nowadays men only wear traditional dress in a handful of villages.

Maya *Traje*

Traditional clothing connects the Maya to their past and present-day identity. It's the most visible manifestation of the Maya cosmovision and resistance to colonization. "Fabrics are the books the colonists could not burn" has become a political slogan. Nobel Prize laureate and indigenous rights leader Rigoberta Menchú states: "Our women have known how to struggle for our culture. It's women who preserve the art of weaving; we are the weavers. Our knowledge concerning weaving, our art is very advanced. That's why many people everywhere consider the Guatemalan woman to be an artist. And weaving is an art."

Each design is associated with a particular village, and more than a hundred and fifty Guatemalan towns are documented as having distinctly different *traje*. The designs use combinations of colors, abstract shapes, words, animals, and plants. From the ancient Maya cosmovision come symbolic representations of the sun, moon, butterflies, bats, and serpents. The quetzal bird is a popular motif, as it's considered the spiritual protector of the K'iche' kings; legend has it that it stopped singing after the Spanish came, and its red chest represents the blood spilled by the conquistadors.

The standard outfit for most Maya women in rural areas includes a colorful *huipil*, a loose blouse made from three woven and embroidered panels decorated with ribbons or decorative stitching, and a *corte,* a wrap-around skirt that reaches to the shoes and is secured with a *faja*, a woven belt or sash. To cover the head and protect from the sun, women wear a *tzute*, a folded textile that can also be used to strap a baby to their back.

In Nebaj, a town high in the Altos Cuchumatanes mountains, the women's *traje* is one of the most eye-catching in Guatemala. It consists of a red skirt with yellow stripes, a woven belt, a heavily embroidered *huipil*, an all-purpose shawl, and an elaborate headdress woven into the hair.

In contrast, the women of Santiago Atitlán wear a *huipil* of purple-striped white cloth embroidered with fanciful motifs and figures of animals, birds, and flowers. The most striking feature of their costume is the *tocoyal*, a textile wrapped around their head like a turban, which appears on the 25-centavo coin.

In San Juan Atitlán, another mountain village, both men and women are commonly seen in traditional *traje*. The men wear a red *camisa* (shirt) with a long squared-off collar, the ends of which are stitched to be used as pockets. Over the red shirt, a black or dark brown

A local artisan produces textiles using a backstrap loom.

capixay (tunic) is held in place by a *faja* (sash). The pants are white and plain and the ensemble is usually topped off with a straw hat and a festively decorated *moral* (shoulder bag).

The weaving, wearing, and preservation of traditional *traje* is seen by many Maya as essential to their existence. Many cooperatives of weavers in different regions are fighting against the increasing commercialization and appropriation of their textile traditions by foreign designers and fashion firms, and have called for their unique designs to be protected under copyright law.

THE BACKSTRAP LOOM

To create their unique *trajes*, tapestries, and textile artworks, indigenous weavers use a backstrap loom. This seemingly simple setup can create incredibly elaborate patterns, using just half a dozen wooden rods. To use the loom, the weaver attaches one end to a house post or tree, and wraps a belt at the other end around her hips. Sitting on the ground, she can then lean back to keep the warp taut for weaving, or sit forward to release the tension in a rocking motion.

This kind of weaving has not changed in over four thousand years and is intrinsically linked to a sense of identity by the Maya and other indigenous groups.

CHAPTER SIX

TIME OUT

Family gatherings and fiestas are frequent in Guatemala, and much time is spent talking to neighbors. During the hotter months, you will see entire families at the public swimming pools and barbecuing. It seems that Guatemalans are always glad to find an excuse for a party—to celebrate birthdays, weddings, baptisms, church confirmations, *quinceañeras*, anniversaries, and many more events—quite apart from the many holidays and fiestas in the villages and cities.

MEETING UP

In the large cities there are all types of bars and cafés where people meet for drinks. There are many popular discos where friends meet to dance salsa, merengue, and combined versions of blended hip-hop. Cinemas are found only in large cities, and typically show only films produced in the US.

Friends taking a selfie.

In all of Guatemala's cities and towns, especially the smaller ones, the central square is of the utmost importance. This is the vital heart of the place, where people meet and stroll, and where weekly or monthly markets are held. The Sunday saunter through a city park or town center is a universal pastime. The verb for this particular activity is *dominguiar*, "to Sunday," which means to meander around in a leisurely, aimless fashion on a Sunday. Even at other times, it's common to see all ages "hanging out" in groups, sitting on the benches, on blankets, or on the park wall. Young people will meet up there for evening outings. The central plaza is also the site of most political demonstrations.

In the larger cities, there are shopping malls where Ladinos and Maya alike enjoy window-shopping and strolling. It's common to see entire families casually walking through the malls on weekend evenings.

FOOD

Guatemalan food can be categorized as typical Maya, urban Ladino, and African-influenced Garífuna cuisine, although there are some standard dishes, such as tortillas and beans, that occur throughout the country. In general, the food in Guatemala is adequate, but it should not be the primary reason for a visit.

For the typical Maya family, food comes from their own homegrown crops or what they trade at market. Maize is the primary staple, and every Maya woman knows how to make tortillas, which are cooked on a clay platter (comal). These are usually flat and round, but can be shaped into all sorts of forms such as logs, balls, and so on. Tortillas are eaten at almost every meal, accompanied by some form of black beans—soup, refried paste, puréed, with rice, and so on. Vegetables are also common fare, especially squash, tomatoes, hot chilies, and hot peppers.

Specialty dishes eaten in the Guatemalan highlands include *pepián*, a unique chicken stew flavored with pumpkin seeds, hot chilies, and tomatoes, and *pinol*, a chicken-flavored corn mush. Other Maya dishes include *caldos* (stews made with different types of meats), *fiambre*, which is a special salad of meats and vegetables served on All Saints' Day (November 1), and *mosh* (a porridge of oats and milk eaten for breakfast).

For Ladino Guatemalans, the food is a combination of Mexican, US, and European cuisine, although many still eat traditional Maya food as well. Steak, hamburgers, chow mein, rice, and fries are all common foods. German-style sausages and Italian-style pizza and pasta are also readily available. Ceviche is more common on the coasts. Some

Top to bottom: A woman preparing tortillas; Guatemalan dish *platanos en mole*—plantain in a thick chili and chocolate sauce; tied tamales.

Ladinos, especially rural folks, commonly follow a Maya diet primarily composed of frijoles, tortillas, cheese, cream, chili, and coffee. *Carne asado* (charcoal-broiled fillet of beef), *chicharrones* (fried pork rinds), *chiles rellenos* (meat-stuffed peppers), and tamales (little filled dough pies) are all widespread favorites.

Garífuna cuisine is more tropical in nature and has African roots. Bananas, coconuts, and seafood are commonly used in recipes in and around the coastal area of Lívingston. Fried plantains are also a well-known food across Guatemala that were originally made popular by the Garífuna.

DRINK

Coffee

Blessed by rich volcanic soils, Guatemala produces some of the best shade-grown mountain coffee in the world, and has done so since coffee took off as an export product in the 1850s. In the past, almost all of the best beans were exported abroad and the locals—unless they lived on a coffee farm—had to make do with instant coffee or a rough roast. That situation has changed dramatically, especially in Antigua and Guatemala City, where specialist coffee shops and bars offer bean-to-cup experiences for coffee lovers from all over the world. The eight coffee-growing regions are Antigua, Acatenango Valley, Conbán, Atitlán, Huehuetenango, Fraijanes Plateau, Nueva Oriente, and San Marcos; and the harvest takes place from October to February. Many farming cooperatives in the towns around Antigua offer coffee farm tours where you can see how the coffee beans are harvested and processed and get an immersion into the lives of the small-scale farmers and their families who work the fields.

Fruit Juices and Smoothies

Guatemala produces a wealth of exotic fruits alongside *mora* (blackberries) and *fresa* (strawberries). Local markets are stacked with colorful displays of fruit and also have juice stands where you can mix and match juiced fruits like *moreish* (mango), purple *pithaya* (dragon fruit), creamy *guanabana* (soursop), and endemic specialties like *nance* (hogberry), with *zanahoria* (carrot), *remolacha* (beetroot), and *avena* (oats). Often these juices will be served in a plastic bag with a straw.

Liquados (smoothies) are a delicious way to combine fruits and are made with water (*con agua*), or for a few quetzales more, with milk (*con leche*). Guatemalans have a sweet tooth and will automatically throw in a large spoon of sugar when making *liquados*, so clarify you want it *sin azucar* (without sugar) when you order. Water purity can be a problem in Guatemala and the best stands will use bottled water (*agua pura*), but it is always best to check.

All the usual brands of sodas, colas, and other fizzy drinks (*gaseosas*) are available alongside local versions, which again tend to be served in a plastic bag at street stalls.

Beer

With a distinctive stylized rooster on the label and a simple yet effective slogan declaring it "*La Mejor Cerveza*" (The Best Beer), Gallo is the most popular lager in Guatemala and has been in business for over a hundred years. Dominating the local market, it is a fresh-tasting blonde beer that is best served cold and perfectly accompanies the spicy stews of the highlands. Less popular in terms of sales but deeper in flavor is Cabro, a lager which like Gallo is also sold in both small bottles and one-liter bottles. Moza, a dark bock-style beer, is produced by the same brewery as Cabro.

There's a strong craftbrew scene in Antigua at places like the Antigua Brewing Company, a microbrewery and bar that serves a rotating combination of small-batch IPAs, Belgian blondes, and stouts. Guatemala City also has a burgeoning craftbrew community, with its heart in the hip-and-happening restaurant and bar zone of 4 Grados Norte in Zona 4.

Spirits

Rum lovers come to Guatemala for the award-winning aged rums produced by Zacapa Centenario, a local company now majority-owned by drinks giant Diageo. Instead of molasses, Zacapa uses *guarapo* (sugar cane juice) in its distillation process, which takes place on the coast. The distilled spirit is then aged at altitude at Zacapa's warehouse in Quetzaltenango in oak barrels that have previously held oloroso sherry, French cognac, and US whiskies. This creates a greater range of flavor profiles in Zacapa's premium sipping rums that is also enhanced by the solera process of blending six- to twenty-five-year-old rums.

The other major rum producer is Botran, also based in Quetzaltenago, which produces white rums for cocktails and aged rums for sipping.

Botran also produces the popular and very inexpensive Quetzalteca, an *aguardiente* (literally "firewater") that features on the label an eye-catching depiction of an indigenous girl with braided plaits and an embroidered huipil. Quetzalteca can be purchased at any small *tienda* (store) or gas station, and comes in small bottles that can be stashed in a pocket. Flavored versions include *agua de jamaica* (hibiscus) and *tamarindo* (tamarind).

Among the Maya, especially in the northern hills, village fiestas are the time to drink *cusha*, a fiery Maya moonshine made by distilling a mash of maize and *panela* (artisan cane sugar) in homemade stills. Cusha can vary in quality and should be approached with caution.

The Garífuna communities of Livingston have their own version of aguardiente called *gifiti* or *guiffity*, often steeped in medicinal herbs that give it a slightly bitter taste and a reputation—touted by vendors—as a strong aphrodisiac.

EATING OUT

Restaurant fare in Guatemala will vary according to the size of the city or town. There is a distinction between a restaurant and a *comedor*, which is an inexpensive café serving simple food, popular with locals.

There are a number of American fast-food restaurants in the cities (McDonald's, Taco Bell, and Pizza Hut are the most common) and, surprisingly, a growing number of Chinese restaurants. In the larger

TIPPING

Guatemalans generally don't tip, and certainly not at street stalls, cafés, or the low-cost lunchtime *menú del día* restaurants that serve a set menu of soup, entree, and drink. At fancy restaurants or in places like Antigua, where large numbers of foreign expats call home, you can expect a more US-style tipping culture. But generally, it's not like the US, where leaving a gratuity is virtually obligatory.

That said, many Guatemalans rely on a *propina* (tip) to supplement a meager income, and the kids who help pack groceries at the supermarket will appreciate some small change in return for their services, as will the marimba group livening up a restaurant or picnic area.

For hotel staff, such as bellboys and maids, calculate tips of around US $1 and upward depending on your generosity and budget.

Tour guides may be on very low salaries, especially indigenous guides in remote areas, and a US $10 tip or higher, depending on the size of the group, will be much appreciated.

There is no need to tip taxi drivers, but always agree on a price before setting off, then stick to it. If you hire a driver for multiple days or exclusively use the same taxi, then a tip for punctuality and speedy service will encourage more of the same.

cities, good restaurants of all types can be found, although price does not necessarily correlate with the best food or service.

Guatemala is a country of meat-lovers, and vegetarians should be warned that there is not much vegetarian fare. Chicken is a favorite dish, and chicken restaurants are ubiquitous. The Pollo Campero chain, for example, is so popular that Guatemalans often transport large packs of Pollo Campero chicken across the border to relatives living in the US. *Churraso* (charcoal-grilled steak), barbecued meat (often open air), and *chicharrones* (pork crackling) are also Guatemalan carnivore delights that can be found in restaurants and at street vendors.

SHOPPING FOR PLEASURE

In many ways, Guatemalan life revolves around shopping, whether that includes a daily trip to the *tiendita del esquina* (corner store) or a grocery shop, a trip in the back of a pickup to browse the stalls of produce and livestock at a weekend market in the highlands, or window shopping at one of the shiny new state-of-the-art shopping malls in Guatemala City.

The vast Oakland Place mall in Zone 10 of Guatemala City is like a trip back to the US in the 1980s, when the mall was everything. It's equipped with food courts, cafes, restaurants, and a cineplex.

Guatemalan crafts (known locally as *artesanía*) are very popular with tourists. Each artistic tradition is localized, with different regions and sometimes

A Maya grocery market.

individual villages specializing in particular crafts. These handmade products are exquisite, with the most well known being the colorful woven textiles that are sold all over the world. Other local crafts include the wool and blankets of Momostenango, the reed mats made near Lago de Atitlán, and rope crafted in Cotzal and San Pablo la Laguna. Other villages have specialties in pottery or flowers.

It's best to purchase Guatemalan crafts in their places of origin, both because the quality is likely to be better and because this ensures that the locals get more of the profit. However, good selections can be found in the local markets or in tourist locations.

WORRY DOLLS

Made in the highlands from scraps of off-cut textiles that are shaped around wood or wires, *muñecas quitapenas* (worry dolls)—also known as *quitapesares*—are colorful inch-tall figures that are believed to help children and adults sleep. The idea is to confide your worries to the doll before bedtime and then place it under your pillow. The doll then takes on the worry while you drift into a relaxing sleep.

They come in packs of six to cover Monday to Saturday, as even worry dolls need a day off.

The tradition is thought to be linked to the ancient Maya belief that humans can communicate with the gods through intermediaries, a belief that still informs Maya shamanistic practices today. One local legend states that the dolls represent the Maya goddess of maize, Ixmucané, who was responsible for crafting the first people from maize after receiving a special gift from the sun god that allowed her to resolve any problem a human could face. By whispering to the doll, it's said, you are communing with the goddess.

Especially popular with children, these small interesting gifts are now sold all over Guatemala. Seek out handmade ones up in the highlands, where Maya traditions are still strong.

MONEY MATTERS

The national currency of Guatemala is the quetzal (Q), named after the national bird, which the ancient Maya so revered and whose flame-red tail feathers were highly valued and used as currency. One quetzal is worth 100 centavos and the Banco de Guatemala issues notes in denominations of 1, 5, 10, 20, 50, 100, and 200 quetzales. Coins of 1, 5, 25, 50 centavos, and 1Q are in circulation, but apart from 1Q are close to worthless.

The quetzal was adopted as the new currency in 1924, during the government of President José María Orellana (who appears on the 1 quetzal note), replacing the peso. Many Guatemalans, however, still refer to pesos when asked for prices, which can be confusing for foreign visitors negotiating a new currency.

You might also hear people referring to *pisto*, a slang word for cash, or *plata* (literally "silver") instead of *dinero* (money). A useful phrase to remember if street vendors persistently pursue a sale despite your polite refusal is: "*Pisto no hay!*" (No cash!).

Most top-end hotels, stores, and restaurants will accept credit card payments or US dollars in Guatemala City, Antigua, and other tourist spots, but you will need quetzals in smaller denominations for street food, transport, and other daily expenses. You can exchange cash at street stores called Casa de Cambio (Exchange Bureau) or Cambio de Divisas (Foreign Currency Exchange), but they often insist on pristine dollar bills, just as hotels and stores do.

The easiest way to get quetzales is by withdrawing cash using your credit card or debit card at an ATM run by a bank like Banco Industrial, one of the largest. Always cover the keypad when tapping in your PIN, and use ATMs located inside banks when possible. In remoter areas of the country, you may not have access to an ATM, so stock up on *billetes* (bank notes) before you go.

SPORTS

Soccer

More than a popular sport, *futbol* is like a religion for Guatemalans. Anywhere there's a ball and a dirt field, kids will get together for a *chamusca*, an informal kick-about. Guatemalans follow the soccer news avidly, both local and international. Guatemala City has the largest soccer stadium in Central America and the top clubs are Municipal, Comunicaciones, and Antigua.

Guatemala has never qualified for the World Cup, but during the tournament people will wake at all hours of the night to catch the games, and will usually support another Latin American team. The country does have a World Cup record as well. Guatemalan striker Carlos Ruíz, nicknamed "*El Pescadito*" (The Little Fish), played in five World Cup qualifiers between 2002 and 2018, scoring thirty-nine goals. That is more goals than any other player in the history of the World Cup, and three more than the fabled Cristiano Ronaldo. He also holds the record for the number of appearances for the national side, and is the all-time leading scorer in the Liga Nacional de Fútbol de Guatemala (National Football League of Guatemala). Now retired, his international career took him to Major League Soccer in the US, where he played for the LA Galaxy and FC Dallas.

PITZ (POK TA POK)—REVIVAL OF THE ANCIENT BALL GAME

The pre-Columbian civilizations of Mesoamerica played a ritualized ball game that was linked to human sacrifice. In the creation myth of the Maya, the Popol Vuh, the game plays a key part in the story of the hero twins Hunahpu and Xbalanque, who go down into Xibalba (the Maya underworld) to avenge the death of their father at the hands of the underworld gods by beating them in this game. Played with a heavy rubber ball by two teams who could only strike the ball with their hips, it was both a sport played for points and a stylized ritual that could end in the decapitation of the losing side. In the ancient Maya city of Tikal alone, five ball courts have been excavated.

More recently, the game has been revived in Maya communities in Mexico's Yucatan peninsula, where it's called pok ta pok, and in Maya regions in Guatemala, where it's called pitz. It's a source of pride that this ancient custom continues, and is considered a form of honoring their ancestors. Modern games start with a ritual by a Maya healer who burns copal incense and blesses the ball and players with the smoke before play can commence.

Nowadays, the losers may feel deflated but leave with their heads. Guatemala's young pitz players compete nationally and the best teams earn a place at the Pok Ta Pok World Cup, where they play against teams from Mexico, Belize, El Salvador, and Panama.

Olympics

Guatemala first competed at the Olympic Games in 1952, but its first medal didn't come until the 2012 Games in London, when Érick Bernabé Barrondo García walked away with the silver medal at the Men's 20 km Racewalk.

The country was temporarily banned from participating at the 2024 Olympics after the Guatemalan Constitutional Court challenged the statutes of the country's National Olympic Committee. The ban meant that Guatemalan athletes were not able to participate as a team or march with the flag. After much negotiation, and a personal meeting between the International Olympic Committee and newly elected President Bernardo Arévalo in 2024, the suspension was lifted.

Guatemala went on to have its best Olympics ever in Paris, with a gold medal and Olympic record for Adriana Ruano Oliva in women's trap shooting, and a bronze medal for Jean Pierre Brol in men's trap shooting.

Hiking

There are many hiking trails across the country, with popular treks up active volcanoes, trails through dense rainforests alive with the sound of frogs, birds, and howler monkeys, and multi-day hiking and camping trips to remote archeological sites.

One of the easiest volcano hikes is to Volcán de Pacaya, just outside Guatemala City, where you can explore the lava fields and roast marshmallows over hot rocks before walking to the summit. The nine-hour trek to the top of Acatenango, Guatemala's third highest peak at 13,041 feet (3,976 meters), is definitely one of the most exhausting and exciting treks in the country, and for safety should be done with a reputable guide or trekking company in Antigua. After six hours of slogging up relentlessly steep slopes, hikers reach the base camp, where they spend the night and enjoy spectacular views of the nearby Volcan de Fuego, which is in a state of almost continuous eruption. The last two hours to the top is done before the break of dawn the next day to appreciate the sun rising above a sea of clouds.

Tajumulco is the highest peak in Central America at 13,850 feet (4,222 meters) above sea level. Best tackled from Quetzaltenango, the hike to the summit of Tajumulco is fairly easy apart from the altitude and can be tackled without a guide. However, reaching the trail takes you through an area where opium poppies were once the staple crop and where land disputes between the municipalities of Tajumulco and Ixchiguán have sometimes flared into violence. Traveling with an experienced tour operator like Quetzaltrekkers is recommended, as they offer a two-day trek with camping on the volcano that starts early on day two, to reach the summit before sunrise. Quetzaltrekkers also offers a five-day trek from Nebaj to Todos Santos over the pine-covered Cuchumatanes mountains.

One of the longest and most rewarding hikes in Guatemala is the five- or six-day route through the dense Petén rainforest from Carmelita, a three-hour drive from Flores, to the Maya ruins of El Mirador, one of the oldest and most extensive Maya cities, and home to La Danta, the largest pyramid by volume in the world. The only other way to get there is by helicopter.

Baseball, Basketball, and Boxing

Béisbol (baseball) is a popular sport in Guatemala and is organized by Fedebeis Guatemala, the Baseball Federation of Guatemala. The national team has competed in the Pan American Games and the Central American and Caribbean Games but has never produced an MLB major leaguer. *Baloncesto* (basketball) is also popular in schools, colleges, and the national level, with male and female teams representing each departmental capital. The Guatemala national basketball team is administered by the Guatemalan National Basketball Federation (FNBG). Guatemala is the most populous nation in the Americas that has never qualified for a major international basketball event. The country's most famous basketball player is the singer Ricardo Arjona, who played for the national team and for many years held the national record for the most points scored in a basketball game, 78.

Amateur and professional *boxeadores* and *boxeadoras* (male and female boxers) practice *el boxeo* (boxing) at gyms around the country, with young hopefuls and old pros embracing the sport of kings. Fans avidly follow the fights of young boxers like the super middleweight Lester Martinez, who has put Guatemala on the boxing map, and the pioneering female boxer Maria Micheo who has inspired many young women to pull on gloves and follow her into the ring.

One place where the gloves are definitely off is the K'iche' village of Chivarreto in San Francisco el Alto in Totonicapán. Every year on Good Friday since at least the year 1900, a boxing ring is erected in the village square for a slugathon of bare-knuckle boxing that only gets messier as the boozed-up competitors—who consider training to be for wimps—fight it out until there is one man standing.

Cycling

Ciclismo (cycling) is a highly popular sport in Guatemala, and road racing, mountain biking, and BMX are practiced for sport and enjoyment. Tourists who want to see the country on two wheels also come to test themselves on highland roads, or at a slower pace, savoring scenic panoramas from the saddle.

The highlight of the cycling year is the Vuelta de Guatemala road race organized by the Federación Guatemalteca de Ciclismo, which began in 1957 and has been won by cyclists from Guatemala, Colombia, Spain,

Costa Rica, and Mexico, although Guatemalans have dominated the race in the last decade. Held at the end of October and beginning of November, the Vuelta has ten stages covering a grueling 750 miles (1,200 km) of steep climbs up highland roads at lung-busting altitudes, which attracts world-class international competitors. The Vuelta Ciclistica Internacional Femenina a Guatemala is a shorter 50 mile (75 km) road race for elite female cyclists.

Surfing

With few established surf spots along its black-sand Pacific strip, and a predominance of beach breaks rather than point breaks, Guatemala is only now gaining a reputation among surfers. One of the main beaches for advanced surfers is Champerico, a two-and-a-half hour drive from Quetzaltenango. Itztapa in Escuintla Department has a rivermouth break that can get big waves. The two most popular beaches with locals and foreign surfers are the party-town newcomer El Paredon, which is backed by dense forest, and Monterrico, which is reached by ferry from La Avillana. International surf competitions have been held in Guatemala at Itztapa and Playa Hawaii, near Monterrico, but are still quite low-key in comparison to the pro surf competitions that take place in neighboring El Salvador, with competitors mainly coming from Central and South America. The Asociación Nacional de Surf de Guatemala, or Asosurf, organizes competitions and local rankings and is recognized by the International Surfing Association (ISA).

THE ARTS

Visual arts

Guatemala has a rich artistic heritage that stretches back
to the Olmec period, some two thousand years ago. This
was when the giant stone heads and pot-bellied statues of
Monte Alto—currently in the central park of La Democracia
in Escuintla—were made, and a distinctively Olmec style
of carving was used in the ancient city of Tak'alik Ab'aj,
declared a UNESCO World Heritage Site in 2023.

The Olmec period was followed by the elaborately
decorated polychrome ceramics, jade jewelry, and
inscribed stone sculptures of the ancient Maya. These
artistic treasures can be appreciated *in situ* at the
magnificent UNESCO sites of Tikal and Quiriguá, but
the best and most diverse collections of ancient Maya art
are found in the Museo Popol Vuh and the beautifully
refurbished Museo de Arte Maya in Guatemala City.

Following the Spanish conquest, the colonial period saw
the construction of sturdy Catholic convents and churches
like the Iglesia La Merced that can still be appreciated
today in Antigua, with embellished baroque exteriors,
glittering gilded altars, religious statues, and emotive
paintings of saints. The Museo Nacional de Arte Colonial
in Antigua, housed in the old Universidad de San Carlos,
is a window into Guatemala's colonial past, and has a
fine collection of baroque paintings by Tomás de Merlo
(1694–1739).

The 1920s and '30s saw the rise of *indigenismo*, a
movement that focused on indigenous culture and rural
scenes but in a Modernist style. Alfredo Gálvez Suárez
(1899–1946), who studied in Mexico with the muralists

José Clemente Orozco, Diego Rivera, and David Alfaro Siqueiros, painted a mural in the Palacio Nacional that depicted the violent *choque* (clash) of two civilizations during the Spanish conquest of the Maya kingdoms in present-day Guatemala.

The country's most famous artist is Carlos Mérida (1891–1994), who met and was influenced by Pablo Picasso and other European artists in Paris, before moving to Mexico where he mingled with the country's muralists and developed a semi-abstract style of painting that incorporated Maya myths and cosmology. Artist Margarita Azurdia (1931–1998) has also explored abstraction and surrealism in a series of works inspired by the deities and animal characters in the Popol Vuh.

Modern Maya art starts with painters like Andrés Curruchich (1891–1969), who in the 1930s turned to watercolors and oil paints to produce detailed scenes of the Kaqchikel Maya, and their typical *trajes*, markets, feast days, and rituals in his hometown of San Juan Comalapa. Curruchich was lauded in the US in the 1950s as a talented naif painter. Back home he trained some five hundred painters and artisans in San Juan Comalapa—now known as the "Florence of America"—and helped launch a folk art movement that has spread to many Maya towns and villages.

Today, the most famous contemporary Maya artist from San Juan Comalapa is Paula Nicho Cúmez. Her surreal depictions of indigenous women are painted using the colors and motifs of the local *huipil* blouses, and combine magical folk stories from her Kaqchikel upbringing, her dreams of taking flight, and her own strong views on female empowerment.

Tz'utujil artist Antonio Pichillá (b. 1982), from San Pedro La Laguna on Lago de Atitlán, explores the spiritual cosmology of the Maya, their weaving traditions, and their resistance to European colonialism to produce striking conceptual pieces that have been exhibited in museums and galleries around the world.

Music

Whether it is traditional Maya musicians playing flutes, drums, and conch shell trumpets to accompany sacred rituals, a *cumbia* band getting hips to swing with saxophones and an electric piano at a village fiesta, a Led Zeppelin tribute band rocking out in an Antigua dive bar, or homegrown legend and Latin pop-rock icon

A typical marimba dance orchestra, performing in Antigua.

Ricardo Arjona leading a sing-along of his greatest hits in a soccer stadium, Guatemala is awash with music. No chicken bus ride is complete without the driver blasting out his favorite tunes for the duration, with all the cumbia, *norteño*, salsa, bachata, reggaeton, and mariachi music you hear elsewhere in Latin America.

Marimba

The plinky-plonk of the marimba is the soundscape to Guatemala and a deeply ingrained reflection of Guatemalan identity. It is as ubiquitous in shiny city shopping malls and restaurants as it is in Maya fiestas or at wedding receptions.

First brought to Central America from West Africa by slaves in the sixteenth century, the early marimba was adapted by the Indigenous Maya and adopted into their rituals and ceremonies in the 1700s. The key moment for the marimba boom came in Quetzaltenango in 1894 when marimba builder and player Sebastián Hurtado added a row of extra keys (equivalent to black keys on a piano) so band leader Julián Paniagua Martínez could play the popular dance tunes of the time.

A wooden xylophone-style instrument, the Guatemalan marimba has rows of wooden keys that are struck with mallets to produce different notes assisted by wooden resonators that hang below the keys.

Depending on the size, the marimba is usually played by three or four *marimbistas*, each using two mallets in each hand. Popular dance orchestras like Marimba Chapinlandia usually perform with two marimbas, drums, stand-up bass, and maracas.

The country's unofficial anthem is "Luna de Xelajú," a soulful love song composed by Francisco "Paco" Pérez in 1944 that is considered a classic instrumental for Guatemalan marimba. Declared Guatemala's national instrument in 1978, the marimba is a source of pride and nostalgia for Guatemalans everywhere. The Marimba Chapinlandia band, founded by composer Froilán Rodas Santizo (1922–2004), is the most famous of the big marimba dance bands, and they continue to enchant audiences under the leadership of his son Froilán Rodas Santizo Jr.

Pop and rock

There is no Guatemalan musician or singer more famous than the Latin king of the soft-rock ballad, Ricardo Arjona, a former basketball player and school teacher born in Jocotenango, just north of Antigua. With three decades of hit records and over 20 million albums sold, Arjona announced in 2023 that he was taking a break from touring due to back pain, but his storytelling songs continue to attract millions of listeners on Spotify. While many of his poetic ballads are love-torn tales of heartbreak, he has also tackled social issues such as the secret thoughts of a young person struggling with their gender identity in "Que Nadie Vea" (So Nobody Sees) from 2008, or the plight of Central American and Mexican migrants hoping to enter the US in "Mojado" (Wetback), a song that is as powerful and relevant today as it was in 2006 when it was released.

CHAPTER SEVEN

TRAVEL, HEALTH, & SAFETY

Guatemala is like four worlds in one, with its long Pacific coast separated from its short strip of Caribbean by the jungles of the Peten, and mountainous highlands dotted with volcanoes. Getting around the country is all part of the fun, with tuk-tuks buzzing over cobblestones like enraged wasps, old-school chicken buses with no knee room providing hairpin adventures between highland towns, and modern Pullman buses with the air-conditioning set to Arctic zipping from city to city and on to other destinations in Central America.

Some places like Flores—gateway to the jaw-dropping pyramid temples of Tikal—are best reached by air in a small plane, an adventure in itself. For Livingston on the Caribbean coast, only a boat will get you there, either by sea from Puerto Barrios or neighboring Belize, or up from Rio Dulce on a memorable trip along the river between dense jungle banks. The geographic diversity that makes Guatemala such a magnet for visitors seeking to immerse themselves in its breathtaking panoramas also means that few journeys are straightforward. Even on Lago de Atitlán, it is easier to get a boat taxi from village to village than to drive.

Luckily for travelers, transport costs are reasonable compared to neighboring countries like Mexico, and if you plan ahead and heed advice on the hotspots to avoid, travel for foreign visitors is easy to organize and richly rewarding.

GETTING AROUND

By Air

The main gateway to the country is La Aurora International Airport, on the outskirts of Guatemala City. There are direct flights from a little under a dozen cities in the US, with more routes expected to open as tourism numbers grow.

Canadian travelers can transfer through a US hub or Mexico City, while Europeans can also fly via a handful of cities there.

For visitors from the US, Canada, the UK, and Europe, no visa is needed when entering by air, but always check as this can change. Tourists can enter for ninety days, which can be extended by up to ninety days more at the offices of the Instituto Guatemalteco de Migración in Guatemala City.

Taking an internal flight is the fastest and most comfortable way to travel from Guatemala City to Flores, the gateway to the Maya ruins of Tikal. Flights take fifty minutes and both Avianca and TAG cover the route. Be advised, these flights are heavily overbooked on the main holidays of Easter and in the summer holidays.

If you take a flight, you can leave Antigua in the morning and be in Tikal in time for an evening tour.

By Boat

On Lago de Atitlán, fast passenger boats known as *lanchas* whiz you across the water from one pueblo to another like water taxis. Prices are fixed and the *lanchas* leave from a set *embarcadero* (pier). They're supposed to run on a schedule but will generally leave only once full. Always find out the prices before handing over money at the *embarcadero*. A trip from Panajachel to Santa Pedro or San Marcos La Laguna will typically cost you double a short hop to Santa Cruz. There are also private *lanchas* that take individuals and groups on excursions for a negotiated price.

On the Caribbean coast, boats link the laid-back town of Livingston with Puerto Barrios in Guatemala, and Punta Gorda in Belize.

By Road

Buses

The majority of Guatemalans travel by bus, and there are several options to choose from. Premium buses called Pullmans cover all the major routes in Guatemala and travel to San Salvador, Honduras, Belize, Mexico, and other destinations. They vary in quality and comfort but the best have air-conditioning, reclining seats, entertainment, Wi-Fi, and onboard drinks and snacks served by a *tierramoza* (literally "ground stewardess"). Tickets can be bought ahead of time, sometimes online, and buses leave from their own private terminals.

A cheaper, less comfortable, but more adventurous way of traveling is by *camioneta*—the famous "chicken buses,"

A typical *camioneta*, or chicken bus, seen here in Xela.

or *burras* (female donkeys) in local slang. These former US school buses are driven down from the US, pimped out in bright colors, christened with a girl's name, and fitted with a horn loud enough to show the driver means business. They are typically packed full before departing, with people standing in the aisle or hanging off the back, with a great pile of bags tied to the top.

Chicken buses can be uncomfortable, with seats intended for small children, speakers blaring out *norteño* music or reggaetton, and speeds on curving mountain roads that approach death-defying, but they provide an authentic taste of Guatemala you won't get on a Pullman. To add to the chaos, along the route the driver will stop for Evangelists preaching the word, and vendors selling snacks who come on board to peddle their wares. Sometimes on market days in the mountains, you might even see some chickens.

Camionetas have an *ayudante* or *brocha* who helps the driver. These young men shout out the destination, alert the driver to oncoming vehicles while hanging out of the door, and climb the ladder at the back of the bus to load and unload baggage. The *brocha* will pack the bus until it cannot hold another soul, and collect money from everyone by squeezing along the aisle. Always ask locals for the fare to your destination before paying the *brocha*, and check your change.

In many of the larger cities there are minibuses known as *colectivos* that travel within the city for low fares, usually jam-packed with passengers, and stopping when waved down. It can be a bit tricky to figure out the routes for these, but ask locals for advice. In smaller places a *colectivo* might be a taxi that takes multiple passengers, or a pickup truck where you hop in the back and hope it doesn't rain.

Another way of getting around is by using a shuttle bus. Aimed at foreign travelers, these shuttle services offer direct transport between major tourist destinations in small microbuses and vans, and can be booked through backpacker hostels and hotels catering to foreigners. They are considerably more expensive than chicken buses but more comfortable and faster, as they don't stop to pick up additional passengers. Shuttle buses take tourists from Antigua to Xela, Panajachel on Lago de Atitlán to El Paredon on the Pacific coast, Guatemala City to Flores, and anywhere else if there is a big enough group. They even run from Antigua to the Surf City beach of El Tunco in El Salvador.

Taxis

There are taxis in the main towns and the rates are very reasonable, although it's important to agree on a price before you get into the cab, as the majority do not use meters. The rideshare app Uber operates within Guatemala City and Antigua, and between the two cities. Its inter-city routes have also recently expanded to include Guatemala City to Panajachel.

If you want to have a driver for an entire day while organizing your own excursion, you can always negotiate with taxi drivers, but make sure everything is clear before you set out.

Almost every town and village in Guatemala buzzes to the sound of three-wheeled tuk-tuk taxis zipping round the streets. Cheap and ubiquitous, Guatemalans use them to drop kids off at school or transport shopping from the market, for less than a quetzal a trip in many places.

A typical tuk-tuk taxi on the streets of Antigua.

Car Rental

Guatemalans can drive from the age of eighteen. They drive on the right, as they do in the US, and the rules of the road are similar. Drivers and front-seat passengers must wear seat belts. Using a handheld cell phone while driving is not permitted.

If you plan to drive yourself around Guatemala, a number of international and local car rental firms operate at La Aurora Airport, at the border with Belize, and in the main cities. You need to be at least twenty-one to rent a car but people under twenty-five may have to pay a premium. A valid driver's license is essential, either from your own country or an international license, and you must pay with a credit card. Read the contract carefully and factor in any extra taxes and insurance costs, especially liability insurance, which can save you serious expense in the case of an accident.

Always check the brakes, seatbelts, and tires before you leave the rental facility, and make sure there is a working jack (*gato*) and spare tire (*llanta de repuesto*). Note any dents or problems, take photographs or a video to avoid arguments later, and sign everything off with the rental agency before taking the car out.

Renting a car gives you the freedom to explore at your own pace; but with taxis so cheap and driving conditions different from those at home, you may find it easier to pay a local driver to take you out on day trips. This can also avoid any problems if you have an accident, as drivers can be detained by the police until responsibility for a crash is determined.

Petty theft and vandalism can be a problem in some areas. Drive with windows up and doors locked, and always park somewhere safe rather than on the street, such as a car park with security or a hotel parking area. Traveling by car at night is generally not recommended for visitors not used to driving in Central America, but in some areas it's fine. Seek local advice before setting out.

Rules of the Road
In cities, drivers have to be both aggressive to make progress in traffic, and defensive, as other drivers swerve around and cut in front of each other. You have to be aware of taxis, motorbikes, buses, tuk-tuks, and even horses pulling carts, as they all jostle for the limited amount of space. Speed bumps, called *túmulos* (literally "burial tombs"), are a real danger, especially at night. They can be high, and hitting them at speed is not advisable. Potholes and roadworks on some stretches will also test your skills and patience. Outside the cities, the biggest dangers are tightly curving mountain roads, wandering livestock and horses, bicycles without lights, and the blinding high beams of oncoming cars and trucks.

Speed limits vary from 28 mph (50 kph) in towns and cities to 37 mph (80 kph) on rural roads, and 62 mph (110 kph) on highways, although these are regularly ignored. Drivers must be eagle-eyed for road signs that show a sudden change in the speed limit on stretches of road that pass a school.

Traffic cops can give an on-the-spot fine for infractions like speeding. Drivers have fourteen days to pay them at a bank. The police do not have the right to seize your identity documents.

In Guatemalan law you are guilty until proven innocent. In the event of an accident where somebody is injured or killed, drivers can be held in jail and their identity papers and passport retained until liability and damage claims are settled.

Many drivers do not have car insurance, so liability insurance can save a lot of headaches in the event of an accident. Many drivers now use a dashcam so they can produce evidence in the case of a crash.

WHERE TO STAY

Accommodation options in Guatemala range from high-end chain hotels aimed at businessmen to colonial mansions filled with antiques and art in Antigua, and humble homestays with a Maya family in Xela. *Hoteles*, *pensiones*, *posadas*, and *hospedajes* are all names used for various types of hotels, and they come in all categories. You can also rent a luxurious Airbnb with a spectacular view over Lago de Atitlán, a boutique thatched-roof lodge on stilts on the Rio Dulce, a surf camp made from driftwood and palm leaves in El Paredón, or a back-to-basics backpackers hostel in Flores.

A word of warning. Due to narrow plumbing, you are expected to put used toilet paper in the trash can placed next to the toilet when using the bathroom in Guatemala. Bring at least one roll of toilet paper or some tissues along when traveling, as you might not find any in public restrooms.

If traveling by Pullman or chicken bus, make sure you let the driver or his assistant know if you go to the restroom, as some hapless travelers have been left behind while the bus and their bags continue the journey.

PLACES TO SEE

In terms of travel, Guatemala can be divided into seven regions, starting with the capital, Guatemala City, which was once considered a place to stay overnight before a flight but is emerging as a destination in its own right. The colonial gem that is volcano-encircled Antigua is the country's number one destination, followed by the charming and colorful Maya villages nestled on the banks of Lago de Atitlán. For an immersion into the past marvels of the Maya world, fly into Las Flores in the remote Petén region, gateway to the UNESCO site of Tikal and even more remote Maya ruins of El Mirador. The highland city of Cobán in Alta Verapaz is the jumping-off point for visits to coffee plantations and the paradisical pools of Semuc Champey in Lanquín. On the Pacific coast, an emerging surf scene has seen black-sand beach spots like Monterrico, and more recently El Paredón, transformed with backpacker-friendly party hostels and surf schools. Over on the Caribbean side, Livingston is the perfect base for easing into the Afro-Caribbean vibe, and for a visit to the white sands of Playa Blanca, Guatemala's best beach.

The cobblestone streets and colonial treasures of volcano-encircled Antigua are just some of the attractions in this enchanting city, with plenty of charming villages.

If you have more time, go to Quetzaltenango (Xela) and Chichicastenango. If you have a month or more, make sure to explore Livingston and Guatemala's best beaches, or find yourself a laid-back spot on the Pacific and have a go at surfing.

Plaza Cayala, Guatemala City.

Guatemala City

The capital is the major transportation hub both into and out of the country, as well as within it. For most, there is no need to linger in this sprawling city; there are very few sites worth visiting, it's generally dirty, and particular zones can be dangerous for foreign tourists. The city is famous for chaotic crowds and traffic pollution from the seemingly millions of smoke-blowing buses arriving and leaving. Most tourists only stay in "Guate" (as it's called by the locals) for a limited time, using it primarily as a transportation center to get to their next destination.

The cheaper and mid-range hotels are located in Zona 1, while the nicer hotels are in Zona 10. There are expensive restaurants and nightclubs in Zona Viva. There are some interesting museums in Zona 10 and 13, including the Museo Popol Vuh, which contains a good collection of Maya and Spanish colonial art, and the Museo Ixchel, which has a wonderful display of the traditional arts and costumes of Guatemala's highland towns. Maya artifacts can be found in the Museo de Arqueologia y Etnologia, and twentieth-century Guatemalan art in the Museo Nacional de Arte Moderno.

Antigua and Volcano Hikes

This is one of the oldest and loveliest cities in the Americas, located about forty-five minutes by shuttle or private van from Guatemala City. Once the capital of Guatemala, until hit by devastating earthquakes in 1773, it has beautiful colonial buildings, colorful houses, and cobbled streets, set against the backdrop of three large volcanoes. Antigua is especially worth a visit during Semana Santa, the "Holy Week" before Easter, when its streets are covered with bright designs of flower petals and colored sawdust. It's also home to some impressive churches, including La Merced, the Iglesia de San Francisco, and the convent of Las Capuchinas, which is now a museum. A Sunday market is held in Parque Central. Because it's close to Guatemala City, idyllic, and peaceful—as well as being home to many Spanish language schools—Antigua is probably the most visited tourist location in Guatemala.

Panajachel and Lago de Atitlán

Sometimes jokingly called Gringotenango, because of the number of expatriates and foreign tourists who live and visit here, Panajachel is a beautiful and relaxing town to visit. Today, however, it's as popular with Guatemalans and other Central Americans as it is with the long-time residents of North America. About half the population of Panajachel remains non-Guatemalan, and the town has become resort-like in its offerings, with many restaurants, tourist shops, and discos. The adjoining Lago de Atitlán (Lake Atitlán) is a breathtakingly scenic caldera lake—a water-filled collapsed volcanic cone.

"Pana" became known in the 1960s as a sort of hippie haven, with supposed mystical powers coming from vortex energy fields said to be located here. Today there are still many New Agers in the area, making and selling jewelry and other crafts alongside the locals up and down the main streets. Panajachel is the home base for short boat trips to the smaller, mostly indigenous villages of Santiago Atitlán, Santa Catarina Palopo, and San Pedro La Laguna, all surrounding Lake Atitlán.

The pier at Panajachel, overlooking Lake Atitlan.

Xela

Quetzaltenango, known by locals as Xela (pronounced
"Shay-lah"), is the second-largest city in Guatemala. It's
a good place to study Spanish, with numerous language
schools. Also noteworthy are the nearby villages,
which are home to hot springs, small churches, and
handicrafts. The central square is worth a visit as the
main meeting place for young and old, as is nearby San
Francisco El Alto, the largest of all marketplaces
in Guatemala.

Tikal and El Petén

The famous and impressive Maya ruins of Tikal, one
of the world's most beautiful archeological sites, lie
northwest of Flores in the jungle of El Petén. The best
surviving example of Maya civilization at its peak, it
lay forgotten and covered in thick jungle until the mid-
nineteenth century. Plazas, an acropolis, pyramids,
temples, and a museum can be found there. Many of
the pyramids rise high above the tree canopy. There are
many temples to climb in this immense hidden city, and
the views are breathtaking. A wide range of animals can
be seen as well, including howler and spider monkeys,
coatimundi (a relative of the raccoon), parrots and other
tropical birds—including the quetzal, after which the
Guatemalan currency is named—and tree frogs. As an
interesting piece of trivia, Tikal was used to represent
the rebel base in the original 1977 *Star Wars*!

The Caribbean

Home to the Afro-Caribbean Garífuna people,
Lívingston is a tiny tropical outpost that juts out into

the Caribbean with a distinctive culture made up of African, Maya, and European elements. It's located near the Caribbean port of Puerto Barrios and is known for its laid-back charm and way of life, characterized by reggae music, drumming, coconut groves, brightly painted wooden buildings, and fishing. A boat ride on the nearby gorgeous Rio Dulce is an absolute must if you are visiting.

RESPECTFUL TOURISM, PHOTOGRAPHING PEOPLE, AND GIVING BACK

Guatemala is a photographer's dream, with its breathtaking scenery of lakes and volcanoes, and the brightly colored traditional *traje* costumes that differ from village to village. Bustling markets with their stalls stacked with tropical fruit or handicrafts, attended by local vendors in traditional dress, often with their kids helping out, are so picturesque, it is only natural to want to break out your camera and start snapping away. Always keep in mind, however, that responsible tourism is about respecting local people's wishes when taking photographs.

In some villages, you can expect locals to hide from the camera or show strong disapproval if they catch you taking photographs of them or their families, and that should be respected. Be especially careful when taking pictures of children, as this can be misinterpreted by adults who may feel it is exploitative or could lead to the abduction of the child.

If you would like to photograph somebody, instead of sticking a lens in somebody's face, start by making eye contact. Smile. Use the few words you know in Spanish or Mayan. Buy something from a stall. Then you can point to the camera and ask people for permission to take their picture. You may be asked for a couple of quetzals as payment in return. Unless you want to pay, you should politely decline, as it will lead to this practice becoming the norm. Instead, you can show some of the photographs you have taken on your travels, and ask for a WhatsApp number or an Instagram page where you can send people the photographs you have taken of them. (If you do this, make sure to follow through.)

Respectful and positive impact tourism is about making genuine connections with people, and not about getting some good shots and jumping back on the bus.

It's fairly common in tourist locations to be pursued by women and children trying to sell their handicrafts or textiles. If you express an interest, expect other sellers to approach you as well. If you are not interested, just say "*No, gracias*" and walk away.

Often, tourists who visit Guatemala are moved by what they see and the people they meet, and want to give something back. One way to do that is to do a homestay with a local family, knowing that your tourist dollars are going directly to them. Many students arrange homestays while taking Spanish classes in Antigua, Xela, and the highlands. It not only gives you an insight into home life and a chance to practice Spanish, but it builds a personal bond you continue after you leave.

There are many ways to help out if you wish to do so, including volunteering at organizations like the NGO Entremundos Guatemala that works with community tourism groups in Xela, or Houses to Homes, which helps provide houses, education, and healthcare to rural villages around Antigua. There are many church and medical mission programs, and other charitable organizations that offer services and resources to Guatemalans.

It's important to remember that, especially for the Maya, education and preservation of their cultural heritage are priorities.

HEALTH

The main health risk visitors to Guatemala need to try to avoid are contaminated food and water. Drinking contaminated water is the biggest cause of sickness in the country. Even if water appears to be sparkling clean, don't trust it. Always drink bottled water with an unbroken seal. You should also use bottled water to brush your teeth. In restaurants you can ask for *agua pura*, which is another name for purified water. Alternatively, carry a traveler's water bottle like Water-to-Go, which filters out parasites, protozoa, viruses, and bacteria. Contact with contaminated food or water can result in diarrhea that lasts a couple of days, and is best treated with rest and a rehydration drink with electrolytes, or unexpensive charcoal tablets. In more serious cases it can lead to amoebas, giardia, parasites, or gastrointestinal infections. If diarrhea persists or is accompanied by vomiting and dehydration, you can usually find a clinic who will do a stool sample to identify the culprit, and a pharmacy where you can get antibiotics like metronidazole and flagyl to deal with the beastie.

When eating street food, it's best to avoid uncooked dishes like salad and fruit. Stick to hot food straight from the griddle.

There is a moderate risk of contracting malaria in certain regions of the Petén rainforests. Visitors should take an antimalarial medication if they plan to travel to areas of risk.

It's rare to hear of foreigners infected with rabies, which is endemic in Guatemala, but treatment is painful so don't feed stray dogs or pet them.

There is little education about sexually transmitted diseases, including HIV/AIDS (called SIDA in Guatemala). Guatemalans give little regard to safety precautions when it comes to sex, and visitors should use protection if they engage in casual relationships.

Health Services
Like the educational system, the Guatemalan health care system is limited and inadequate. Hospitals and clinics

are underfunded and understaffed. Only about half the population has access to health care. In the large cities, for those who can afford it, good quality medical care is available—there are public and private hospitals and some health centers. There is usually at least one pharmacy in the larger towns and cities. For minor health problems, it's common for a pharmacist to play a diagnostic role and prescribe medication, even antibiotics.

In rural areas, the health situation is worse, with some communities receiving no regular health care or education at all. Folk healing and traditional medicine are commonly used. Most women in the cities give birth in hospitals, whereas women in rural areas are attended by a midwife in their homes.

There are plenty of well-trained doctors in Guatemala and many who speak English. It's usually better to use a private hospital like one of the excellent La Paz Group of hospitals in Guatemala City than a public one. Well-known North American and European prescription medicines are available in local pharmacies, and many do not require a prescription. However, the dosage or instructions may not be clearly stated.

SAFETY

Guatemala has an international reputation for being violent, crime-ridden, and dangerous, but most foreign visitors who take sensible precautions will not encounter any problems. And, as some visitors will point out, visiting Maya sites or colonial cities, or hiking up active volcanoes in Guatemala, is statistically safer than visiting most large cities in the US. Caution should still be exercised in remote rural areas, though, where traveling in a group or on a guided tour is preferable.

Avoid large public gatherings or protests, which in some cases can turn violent. If there are political protests planned during your visit to Guatemala, time your travel to avoid them, as in the past protests have included blockades on major roads.

Petty crime, such as pickpocketing or bag snatching, occurs in Guatemala just as it does elsewhere. (See Tips on Staying Safe on page 162.)

Muggings and carjackings also occur, so visitors should be vigilant and have travel insurance that covers loss. Always submit a police report, but know that it's highly unlikely the thief will be caught or that your valuables will be returned.

Women should avoid traveling to remote areas alone—it's safer to be accompanied by a trustworthy Guatemalan. In general, it's prudent to take precautions by traveling in groups, leaving valuables locked in hotel safes if possible.

Security information for tourist groups, as well as security escorts, are available from ASISTUR, the Tourist Assistance Office of INGUAT (the Guatemalan Tourist Institute) in Guatemala City. They offer 24-hour assistance in English on their phone hotline: dial 1500 or 2290 2810 (or visit asistur.gt/en).

HOT SPOTS TO AVOID

While Guatemala's major tourist centers and beach resorts are generally safe, the departments of San Marcos and

Huehuetenango have been flagged as areas to avoid due to the activities of crime organizations and drug trafficking groups.

In Guatemala City, Villa Nueva is considered a high crime area that should be avoided, as well as Zones 5, 6, 7, 12, 13, 17, 18, 19, 21, and 24.

Travel on buses at night or driving at night in many areas of the country is not advised because of hold-ups.

Before traveling, consult the US State Department's latest Travel Advisory for Guatemala, which gives specific advice for each state.

DRUGS

Of growing concern is the rise of drug trafficking. Reportedly, Guatemala has overtaken Panama in recent years as the new Central American trafficking center. Controlled primarily by Colombian drug barons, the biggest trade is in cocaine, passing through on its way to the United States, followed by opium poppies, which are sold to Mexican traffickers for processing into heroin. In recent years, violence related to the drug trade has increased, especially along the Mexican border. Marijuana is also grown in Guatemala, but is used mainly for domestic consumption. All drugs are illegal in Guatemala, and those who are caught possessing, trafficking, or using any of the above drugs are dealt with severely, receiving long jail sentences or heavy fines.

JUSTICE AND LEGAL SYSTEMS

Money laundering and general corruption continue to be serious problems. Historically, people are wary of approaching the police for assistance. Some believe the police force and the military to be involved with the drug trade, and there are questions about their participation in past civil war atrocities. In recent years, some police officers have been accused of orchestrating criminal gangs and engaging in other criminal activities. Overall, the Guatemalan police force and judicial system are weak and ineffective, and many officers are not sufficiently well trained. Most criminals know that they are unlikely to be caught or punished. It's easy to be impressed by the number of lawyers in Guatemala; however, many Guatemalans are also distrustful of the legal system, which is thought to be susceptible to bribes and corruption.

TIPS ON STAYING SAFE

- Learn some Spanish. The more you can speak and understand, the better.
- Scan your passport, airline ticket, and other documents, and email yourself and your family a copy, along with relevant bank and credit card company numbers in case of theft or loss.
- Travel with others. You are safer in a group. Solo travelers, especially women, can be targeted.

- Don't attract the attention of thieves. Leave gold chains and expensive watches at home. Keep digital cameras and cell phones out of sight.
- Don't use ATMs in the street or at night. Only use ones located inside banks.
- Listen to the locals and heed their advice on places to avoid. Don't enter poor areas of cities and towns. Avoid danger hot spots (see above).
- Know where you are going. Don't wander around with a map out, looking lost.
- Don't flag taxis on the street at night. Have your hotel call you one, ask for the number of a reliable company, or book an Uber.
- Avoid crowds. Don't travel on city buses or visit crowded markets with anything you don't want to lose. Pickpockets take advantage of the crush.
- Use the hotel safe, and have a backup of all your information. Keep emergency money hidden in your belt, shoes, or clothing.
- Don't walk around with all your cash, but do have a small amount you can hand over if mugged. Carry a decoy wallet containing small bills, an expired credit card, and an old library, student, or gym ID for authenticity. If you get held up by an armed assailant, do not resist.

CHAPTER EIGHT

BUSINESS BRIEFING

The potential rewards of doing business in Guatemala are great. It has the second largest population in Central America, the largest economy, and is the largest exporter of goods. It's had the steadiest growth rate in Latin America for over twenty years, and is one of the few countries that experienced growth during the coronavirus pandemic. Today, it's an important regional trade hub with access to markets in North America.

Family-run businesses are still very much the norm, usually focused on one area or product, but there are many startup incentives for switched-on entrepreneurs who are prepared to do their homework.

BUSINESS CULTURE

In Guatemala, who you know and how you come across is nearly as important as the strength of your business proposal. In the past, a small elite of rich families controlled the country. If you wanted to meet the decision-makers and get deals done, you needed an impressive last name or the right friends. While times have changed, the etiquette of doing business still revolves around building personal relationships, which you cannot do by email or with the kind of fly-in-fly-out approach that might work in London or New York.

The key is to get to know the right people, and keep contacts fresh once you've established a connection. Networking and face-to-face contact (in person rather than online) is crucial to the success of any venture you embark upon in Guatemala.

Initial meetings will often ignore the business at hand and revolve around friendly chitchat about your family, your hometown, and what you think of Guatemala. Very often you will need several visits before you see any results. This might be frustrating for foreign executives used to a faster turnaround, but trying to rush negotiations can be perceived negatively, so it's important to slow down and make sure you factor in enough time.

WOMEN IN BUSINESS

Guatemala may be behind the US and Europe when it comes to gender equality in the workplace, but an increasing number of women are represented in the top tiers of conglomerates. Female entrepreneurs are also making their mark in a wide range of industries, including manufacturing, engineering, public relations, marketing, fashion, and design.

Foreign women coming to do business in Guatemala

are unlikely to encounter any problems, although they may sometimes find old-fashioned attitudes to women in some traditional family-run businesses. This is changing, however, as more and more Guatemalan executives are graduating from business schools and universities in the US, and have experience working in multinational corporations.

Whether male or female, when meeting a Guatemalan woman in a business environment for the first time, a warm handshake is the best approach. Once the ice is broken and a good relationship established, an air kiss on the right cheek is normal—but don't attempt it as a foreigner if unsure if a particular situation is appropriate.

SETTING UP A MEETING

If you are approaching a large firm used to dealing with foreign companies, send a direct email or letter in Spanish proposing possible dates for a personal meeting. This should be followed up by an email and phone call about two weeks prior to the meeting to make sure everything is on schedule, and another courtesy call the day before the meeting just to check in and confirm. This might seem like overkill to foreign entrepreneurs, but in Guatemala things can change quite quickly, and businesspeople might be juggling many things at the same time. It's important to keep contacts fresh, remind people you're coming, and build a rapport.

If you want a quick outcome, it's best to come to Guatemala and spend time building contacts, getting a feel for the business landscape, and meeting people in person. Entrepreneurs who have spent months sending out emails from their home country without any concrete response will often find that once in Guatemala, they will start to see results. Guatemalans prefer to deal with people face-to-face, and once they know you personally will be more likely to introduce you to other business acquaintances and help you to set up meetings.

Many business meetings are scheduled in the early morning. Depending on the size of the company, you may be invited to a breakfast meeting with several executives and decision-makers, where you can discuss things over coffee and a pastry. These often act simply as pre-meetings, and are a chance to find out more about you, so don't be frustrated if you don't get straight down to business; this is not the time to get a decision. The same holds true for lunch meetings—a detailed breakdown of your proposal might have to wait until a pitch meeting.

An invitation to dinner, especially on your first night in town, is more likely to be a hospitable gesture and a chance to get to know you better than a chance to get a deal done. Guatemalans are great hosts and will want you to have a good time, but you should remain professional, even when out on the town.

It's usual for the person who issues the invitation to pay the bill. You may offer to pick up the tab, but never offer to "go Dutch" or pay just your share, which is considered rude and tight-fisted. Neither should you insist too hard on paying, as this may also cause offense. It's better to let your host pay and show your appreciation by inviting them out for the next meal.

An important consideration when scheduling meetings is that Guatemalans take their weekends and public holidays seriously, and there is little chance of getting anything done on a Monday morning, a Friday afternoon, or during the long holiday periods around Christmas, New Year's, Easter, or important national holidays (see Chapter 3).

DRESS CODE

Guatemalans are very accepting, but first impressions count, and it pays to dress well for initial encounters. At top-level meetings and business-related social events, formal business attire of dark suit and tie for men and a similarly smart outfit for women are the norm, but elsewhere the rules are more relaxed. The sub-tropical heat dictates the dress code to some extent. For men, a shirt, jacket, and matching trousers are perfectly acceptable, as long as the overall impression is smart; and for women, dresses, skirts, and pants are all appropriate attire. Treat breakfast and lunch meetings as formal unless told otherwise, and dress appropriately for evening events or dinner, depending on the venue.

PUNCTUALITY (OR LACK THEREOF)

The image of Latin America as the land of *mañana* ("tomorrow") portrayed in books, films, and the media is obviously an exaggeration, but even Guatemalans will joke about the local flexibility when it comes to punctuality. The phrase *hora Chapina* ("Guatemalan time") represents the forgiving local attitude to timekeeping, which is natural when dealing with the vagaries of torrential rainy-season downpours, the strength-sapping heat of the dry season, or the peak-hour gridlocks in Guatemala City.

There is also a social aspect. People in Guatemala live in highly interconnected communities. They rely on friends and family much more than in the US or Europe, and set aside time to attend to family issues and social obligations.

In practical terms, a certain amount of leeway should always be factored in when arranging business meetings, to allow for last-minute scheduling hiccups. If you do have to wait, or reschedule a meeting for another day, don't take it personally. It's just a local peculiarity that you will have to get used to. The important thing is not to show undue annoyance when last-minute changes occur, and to make sure you leave room in your schedule for contingencies. Foreigners wanting to do business in Guatemala, however, should always make sure they arrive at the appointed hour for a meeting, and should factor in potential transportation delays when making their plans.

DEALING WITH RED TAPE

Great improvements have been made in recent years to streamline and hasten the process of setting up a business, and most applications can be made online nowadays. There will still be times, however, when dealing with government entities can be frustrating. One way to speed things up is to work closely with a local partner or a reputable agency that already has contacts, and can cut down the time it takes to negotiate the necessary red tape.

For importing or exporting goods through customs, a reputable local agent is essential.

CORRUPTION AND GIFT GIVING

Guatemala has been cracking down on corruption, which in the past has been endemic in politics and has affected the country's image as a safe place to do business. Foreigners doing business in Guatemala should always steer clear of any individual or company that offers a shortcut to official procedures through any form of inducement, whether financial or in kind.

Likewise with gift giving, there are limits. Bringing something typical from your country—attractively wrapped confectionery, a bottle of wine or whiskey, or a coffee-table book featuring glossy photos of your city or country—can act as a nice icebreaker when first meeting potential clients, and is generally considered safe. Equally, a potential client might present you with a bottle of the country's premium Zacapa rum, premium coffee, or chocolates.

Giving gifts and treating clients to hospitality are not illegal, and many businesses will send out small gifts to clients and customers at Christmas. However, it's best not to give expensive gifts that could be misinterpreted as bribes. Some large multinationals operating in the country do not allow staff to accept any gifts, for the same reason.

BUSINESS ATTITUDES

In general, Guatemalans are open and straightforward, and tend to treat business partners as respected friends. They like to make others feel comfortable in both business and social situations and it's common to hear the phrase *no tenga pena* (literally "don't be shy"), which translates as "don't worry." Most Guatemalans strive for honesty, hard work, and personal honor in business deals, as these qualities are highly respected.

Guatemalans can, however, sometimes seem imprudent in their neglect of safeguards or precautionary measures at the planning stage, focusing instead on fixing the problem after the fact. Part of the reason for this attitude is the belief that disasters or problems are acts of God that cannot be prevented. To Westerners this looks like blind fatalism, but remember that this attitude is deeply rooted in Guatemalan culture, and is unlikely to be changed by a well-meaning foreigner.

There are also some Guatemalan businesspeople who believe in the "prosperity theology" of certain Pentecostal Christian denominations, which holds that some people are wealthy because God wants them to be, and others are poor because they lack faith in Him.

It's important to have on-site Guatemalan representatives for any business venture, and it's generally expected that foreigners doing business in Guatemala will visit many times to demonstrate their sincere interest in the people and country. Guatemalan executives emphasize personal contacts with suppliers and partners and like to form long-lasting relationships. They are used to doing business with people from the US, and higher executives and public officials can usually speak English.

Guatemalans like to buy products from the United States, especially if they are inexpensive. Many manufacturing plants inside the country are owned and managed by South Koreans.

HIERARCHY AND STATUS

Guatemalans tend to look for compromise and good relationships in a business setting. They build and focus on personal relationships with people at the same level, but it's clear that orders from above must be obeyed. Among equal-ranking employees, Guatemalans work well together and can be expected to function as a team, but this happens within a strict hierarchical framework. Most Guatemalans look to presenters, trainers, and teachers as the experts; speakers are generally expected to give formal presentations. Most companies are run by an autocratic boss. The hierarchy is not usually based on personal achievement but on social class, education, and family.

One way to increase your own status is to dress well, stay in expensive hotels, and discuss issues that demonstrate your intelligence—not to appear "superior" but rather as curious and open to learning about matters of importance to your hosts (business in Guatemala, its history, and so on).

BUREAUCRACY

Overall, Guatemalans don't like unpredictable and unclear situations when it comes to doing business. They typically emphasize rules, regulations, and controls in the workplace. For this reason, there can be a great amount of bureaucracy, especially in public and governmental offices. It's not uncommon to wait for many hours in a public office before being told that you are in the wrong place, or that you need to come back another day.

As a result, many foreign businesspeople can find themselves running into difficulties: restriction of materials, inadequate communication technology, and rigid working hours (such as the obligatory siesta, and not working in the evenings). In such cases, remember that flexibility is key; don't personalize the situation, and don't get upset about practices that you can't change.

ADDRESSING AND GREETING PEOPLE

When greeting people in a business setting, it's very common for men and women to shake hands, although handshakes are generally gentler, longer, and more limp than in the West. It's appropriate to say "*mucho gusto*" (literally, "much pleasure") when shaking hands. Women sometimes pat each other's right forearm or shoulder instead. Male and female friends often hug and may lightly kiss each other on the cheek or pat each other's back. This is reserved, however, for people who know each other well. When introduced, it's important to smile and make direct eye contact, especially with Ladinos.

On your first introduction to a Guatemalan company or business, when you enter a room you should shake hands with everyone you meet and then again when departing. If you are returning to Guatemala, don't be surprised if people with whom you dealt most on previous visits greet you with a hug and a light kiss on the cheek.

Using titles when addressing people is a sign of respect, and is expected. Use their professional titles: a medical practitioner should be addressed as *Doctor/Doctora*, and anyone with a college degree can be addressed as *Licenciado/a*. Other titles are *Ingeniero/a* (engineer), *Maestro/a* (teacher), and so on. Otherwise, use Mr. (*Señor*), Mrs. (*Señora*), or Miss (*Señorita*), with surnames. You can also use the title without the last name (as simply *Señora, Licenciado, Maestro*, etc.).

Most Guatemalans will have two surnames—their father's, which is commonly listed first, followed by their mother's. Only the father's surname is used when addressing someone. It's considered polite to speak softly and, of course, to engage in social conversation before business.

NEGOTIATING

Business decisions in Guatemala are always made at the highest levels of authority, and chain of command is an important concept. Guatemalans generally try to match businesspeople with others of a similar rank. Because personal contacts and relationships are considered so important, it's usual to begin building the relationship before actual business has started. Likewise, foreign businesses need to offer the same availability in order to build trust with Guatemalans.

When negotiating, it's important that no one becomes overly critical or too direct with regard to other people or companies (even competitors), as this can be off-putting to Guatemalans, and can cause friction and discomfort in interactions.

Guatemalans are inclined to bargain toughly. There is usually a lot of talking during negotiations, and they may take a long time to reach a decision. Some visitors to Guatemala can be surprised by the level of touching and contact in business situations, and incorrectly assume that locals are "schmoozing" in order to close the business deal. However, this is not usually the case but rather a way of demonstrating that you are trusted and well liked. Guatemalans also tend to stand very close to each other when talking—once you get to know people better, they are likely to stand close to you as well.

CONTRACTS

Civil law in Guatemala is based upon legislation and codification. The country has not yet accepted International Court of Justice (ICJ) jurisdiction. In rural Maya areas, it's common for the indigenous people to follow their own time-honored customs and practices, which are respected above the law of the land.

Therefore, contracts in Guatemala are not regarded as sacrosanct. They are generally viewed only as papers, even if they are official and signed by a lawyer. Since breaking a contract is not likely to send anyone to jail, the importance of trust in the business relationship is paramount.

BUSINESS HOURS

For most commercial and industrial businesses, operating hours are from 8:00 a.m. to 6:00 p.m., Monday through Friday. Plants and construction companies start at 7:00 a.m. and usually close between 4:00 and 5:00 p.m. Almost all banks open at 9:00 a.m. and close at 6:00 p.m. and automatic tellers usually close at 8:00 p.m., although some are open all night. Businesses generally observe the holidays mentioned in Chapter 3. During Semana Santa, the week leading up to Easter, little or no business is conducted, and trying to do so may be viewed as insulting.

Many Guatemalan businesses close for siesta time, which occurs in the middle of the day for about two or three hours. It's generally not a good idea to schedule an appointment during this time, because many businesspeople go out for lunch.

Guatemala is in the Central Standard Time zone, -6 GMT (i.e. the same as Chicago), which means that it's one hour behind Eastern Standard Time (i.e. New York). Because the country does not observe daylight saving time, however, for about half of the year it's two hours behind.

CHAPTER NINE

COMMUNICATING

LANGUAGE

The official language of Guatemala is Spanish, although there are at least twenty-two Mayan languages, in addition to Xinca, another indigenous language, and Garífuna, which combines elements of indigenous Arawak and Carib from the Caribbean and Africa with English.

Over 90 percent of the population speak Spanish, and about 40 percent speak an indigenous language as their first language. In some remote areas where indigenous traditions remain strong, where the language of home and the local market is Maya, and where people rarely travel, people may know only rudimentary Spanish. The most common Mayan language is K'iche', while the other Mayan languages spoken include Achi', Akatec, Awakatec, Chalchitec, Ch'ortí, Chuj, Itzá, Ixil, Jacaltec, Kaqchikel, Mam, Mopan, Poqomam, Poqomchí, Q'anjob'al, Q'eqchí, Sakapultec, Sipakapense, Tektitek, Tz'utujil, and Uspantek.

In 2008 the UN declared the Garífuna language—a

combination of Arawak and Carib—a Masterpiece of the Oral and Intangible Heritage of Humanity. After a period of decline, Garífuna communities in Belize, Guatemala, Honduras, and Nicaragua are now working together to keep their language and culture alive.

Speaking Spanish

If you want to meet the locals and learn about their lives, you will need to learn at least a little Spanish. From primary school onward, all Guatemalan children learn English as part of the national curriculum, and some Guatemalans in tourist hotspots will be able to form simple questions such as, "How are you?", "What is your name?", and "Where are you from?" (One of the English questions you might commonly hear in soccer-mad Guatemala is "Which team?") However, unless you are on the Caribbean coast, where English Creole is widely spoken, the only people who will be able to converse with you in English are hotel staff, tour guides, or Guatemalans who have spent some time living in the US.

Being able to deliver a few key phrases, and throw in some local words to break the ice, will not only boost your confidence but will also be greatly appreciated.

Start with a simple greeting like *Hola!* (Hello). When you sit down to a meal, say to the other diners "*Buen provecho*" (Enjoy your meal), and let the cook know that the food was "*Sabroso, gracias!*" (Delicious, thank you!).

If you are asked what you think of Guatemala, you'll get a smile if you say it's "*Chilero!*" which means cool, great, awesome.

Everyday Courtesies

As touched on earlier, having good manners and showing respect for others is very important in Guatemala. When entering a shop or office, people will say to those present "*Buenos días*" (Good morning), "*Buenas tardes*" (Good afternoon), or "*Buenas noches*" (Good evening). A simple "*Buenas*" will do in most situations, whatever the time of day. You can also show respect by addressing or referring to people as *Señor/Señora*, and the elderly as *Don/Doña* with their first name. *Señorita* is the equivalent of Miss in English (there is no equivalent of Ms.). If you don't know a woman's marital status, the best policy is to use *Señorita* with younger women, and let them correct you. When being introduced it's customary to say "*Mucho gusto*" (Pleased to meet you) or "*Un placer*" (A pleasure), then your first name, to introduce yourself.

No Need to Lisp

The first difference you'll notice between Guatemalan Spanish and the Spanish spoken in modern-day Madrid is that there is no lisp on the letters "c" or "z." So, *cerveza* (beer) is pronounced sir-vay-sir, and *gracias* (thank you) is pronounced gra-si-ass.

Guatemalans use *vos* as an informal second person singular pronoun, which is known as *voseo*—as well as *tú*, which is known as *tuteo*. *Voseo* is widespread across Central America, as it is in Argentina and Uruguay. In Guatemala it's used on TV, in ads, and on billboards. One social media campaign aimed at boosting a sense of national pride and inclusion used a mixture of old, young, indigenous, Ladino, and Garífuna Guatemalans to promote the slogan: ¡*Vos también sos Guatemala!* (You too are Guatemala!). If you use the *tú* form it will be understood in Guatemala, but you may find it confusing at first to hear all the *vos* endings on verbs.

As in other Spanish-speaking countries, the formal second person singular pronoun *usted* is used when speaking to elders or superiors to show respect.

Ladinos tend to use the familiar *tú* or *vos* with almost everyone, while Maya when speaking Spanish tend to use the formal *usted* even within the family.

SPEAK LIKE A CHAPIN

Textbook Spanish will help you get by in Guatemala, but to fit in with new friends, using a few local conversational phrases will go a long way. As with most countries, however, use slang expressions with caution, and gauge your audience beforehand. Not all Guatemalans use the same expressions, and a word that provokes mirth among a group of friends might not go over well with others. There are too many *Chapinismos* to list them all, but here are a few you will definitely hear in the street. *Que chilero!*

Bara – a Quetzal
Dame una bara – Give me some money
Bolo – Drunk
Boquitas – Snacks
Burra – Urban bus (literally "donkey")

Cabal – Correct. I agree. You said it.
Canche/a – Blonde or light-haired
Casaca – Lie
Casaquero/a – Liar, smooth talker
Cerote/Cerota – Pal, buddy (literally "cowpatty," traditionally used as an insult to describe a slacker). Sounds rude in translation but you will hear it everywhere, much like American friends calling each other "bro" or "dude." If a friend says it to you, you can say it back.
Chapin/a – Guatemalan
Chucho – Dog
Chumpa – Jacket
Clavo – Problem (literally "nail")
Codo – Tightfisted, mean (literally "elbow")
Colgado como chorizo en tienda – In love (literally "hanging like a sausage in a store")
Dar un jalón – Give somebody a lift in a vehicle
Echar un cuaje – Take a nap
Goma – Hangover
Patojo/a – Child
Pisto – Money
Poporopos – Popcorn
Puchica! – Wow! (said in surprise)
Sho! – Be quiet! Shush! (be especially careful with the context here)
Shuco – Dirty (literally the name of a street food similar to a hot dog)
Shute – Nosey, a busybody
Traida – Girlfriend
Va'a – True, an abbreviation of *verdad*

Learning Spanish

If you plan to spend some time in the country, there are
schools teaching Spanish to foreigners in Guatemala City,
but most visitors head to Antigua, Quetzaltenango (Xela),
and the towns around Lago de Atitlán such as Panajachel,
San Pedro, and San Marcos. As mentioned, many of these
schools offer a package of teaching and accommodation
in a home-stay with a Guatemalan family, which is a great
way to fast-track your Spanish and get a real insight into
the food, culture, and daily life.

Some schools will also offer dancing or cooking classes,
or visits to local communities, as part of the package.

There are many good schools in Antigua, but it's also a
popular city with tourists and foreign expats, so tends to
be more thoroughly Westernized than other locations.
For a more authentic taste of local language, head to Xela.

BODY LANGUAGE

In general, Central Americans in the Northern Triangle
(Guatemala, Honduras, El Salvador) are slightly more
reserved than Costa Ricans or Panamanians when
interacting, particularly in indigenous Maya communities;
but like all Central Americans, they do use body language
to communicate, and it's important to understand the
gestures they use.

One peculiarity you might notice is people pointing
with the lips or the chin. Ask somebody where something
is and they will pucker up and point it out with their pursed
lips. You will also see people scrunching up their nose to
indicate that they don't understand what you are saying.

LEARN SOME MAYAN

There are twenty-two Mayan languages and the most widely spoken one is K'iche', which is also the second most widely spoken language in Guatemala after Spanish. In the villages around Lago de Atitlán, it's a mark of respect to the Maya to know some K'iche' phrases, which are also understood by Kaqchikel and Tz'utujil speakers (although spellings can differ). In K'iche' Maya the stress is on the last syllable, so "thank you" (maltiox) is pronounced mal-tee-OSH. If you only learn one word it should be this one, a term the Guatemalan singer-songwriter Ishto Jueves turned into his most popular song, "Maltiyoox."

Sakarik (sah-kah-rik) – Good morning
Xpek ij (shpek ik) – Good afternoon
Xok aq'ab (shok ak-ab) – Good evening
Tabana utzil (tah-bah-nah oot-zil) – Please
Maltiox (mal-tee-osh) – Thank you
Utz awach? (Oots aw-ach) – How are you?
Utz, maltiox! (Oots mal-tee-osh) – Fine, thank you!

To indicate that someone is being tight-fisted or miserly, it's typical to bend the arm up and tap the elbow, which comes from the expression *No seas codo* (literally "don't be elbow" as a way of saying "don't be tight with money," such as the way the skin tightens when you flex your elbow).

There are two gestures that are considered obscene in Guatemala: when the tip of the thumb protrudes between the top two fingers of a closed fist; and the OK sign, with the thumb and forefinger in the shape of a circle.

Personal Space

In terms of personal space, Guatemalans get quite close with friends and even closer with family (and a ride on a crowded chicken bus on a long journey over bumpy roads is a great way to find out). With foreigners, Guatemalans tend to maintain more distance out of respect, and will only get closer and more familiar as they get to know you.

When meeting male friends, Ladinos will shake hands, and even backslap or bear hug each other. With female friends, an air kiss on the right cheek is common. The Maya are more reserved, and a handshake or a polite nod and a smile is a usual greeting. If they are wearing a hat or cap, they will typically take it off when talking to or greeting someone. Maya women greet each other by extending their right arm and touching the other woman's arm.

Maya Children

Avoid patting Maya children on the head, as the Maya believe it can cause the children spiritual harm or make them ill. Also, as discussed earlier, avoid taking photos of children without asking permission from parents, as it can cause real problems. Rumors of foreigners acting as child traffickers have provoked a violent response in places like Todos Santos de Cuchumatan. In the year 2000, a coach party of Japanese tourists who were taking photos of children were attacked by locals after somebody claimed they were "baby snatchers." One of the tourists and the bus driver died in the incident.

CONVERSATION STYLE

Guatemalans will almost always ask about your family during an initial conversation. They will speak softly, which is considered polite, but this does not mean that they won't be expressive. They are likely to use their hands when talking, and can be animated and dramatic when discussing something emotional. Ladino men especially seem to have a "way with words" and can be especially flattering to women to whom they are attracted.

Guatemalans are happy to talk about geography, history, and culture, but politics and the civil war are not topics you should broach, even if you hear locals criticizing the government. Most Guatemalans do not like a confrontational style and you should avoid direct disagreement in conversation, in that the other person is likely to be offended and go silent. However, they themselves tend to talk over others, and some Westerners are offended by what they feel is continual interruption when talking to Guatemalans, but this is simply a difference of conversational style, more about overlapping than interrupting.

It's important to remain flexible and laid-back in all situations while in Guatemala, but especially when in conversation. If you try to steer a chat toward a specific goal or outcome you will only end up frustrated. You may eventually get there, but it will be after a long period of time and with many non-sequiturs along the way. Personal interactions are what count in Guatemala, and this is reflected in the warm, genuine small talk that is exchanged.

HUMOR

Television is a major source of entertainment, and Guatemalans enjoy watching comedy shows and cartoons. Jokes can be quite earthy, based on puns, wordplay, and double-entendres, many of a sexual nature.

In a group of friends everybody will have a nickname, some funny and some cruel, but all aimed at raising a smile and bonding the friendship. Spend an hour or so in a village market and you will see the smiles and laughter as

Gas station employees sharing a laugh in Flores.

the women stirring steaming pots of stew swap stories and make fun of each other.

In general, Guatemalans, especially the Maya, can come across as more serious when compared to neighbors in Belize or El Salvador. Some Maya women can become embarrassed if they laugh too much. However, the humor is there and for many Guatemalans, laughter is an important way of coping with hard lives and low incomes.

THE MEDIA

There are several major newspapers in Guatemala that can be purchased for less than a quetzal at local roadside stands. The largest and most independent is *Prensa Libre*, a conservative, business-oriented publication that doesn't refrain from challenging the government.

Siglo Veintiuno, its competitor, introduced modern investigative journalism to Guatemala and helped to uncover many cases of corruption and human rights' abuses, but was recently closed down after its founder José Rubén Zamora was jailed for six years in 2022 on corruption charges.

La Hora is an online newspaper. The independent daily *el Periódico* is liberal in its orientation. There are two tabloids. *Al Día* is a colorful mixture of sports, especially football, recipes for making traditional dishes, and gruesome accident pictures. *Nuestro Diario* has the largest circulation and is full of celebrity gossip, sports, and coverage of local news.

The main television channel, Canal 3, broadcasts the national news, with local news programs in larger cities.

A Guatemala City resident catching up on the news in *Soy502*.

Most television channels in Guatemala are controlled by a private Mexican monopoly and offer entertainment rather than information. There are also several Evangelical channels.

Guatemala has several commercial and government-owned radio stations plus evangelical stations. Guatemalan women, especially in the rural areas, love soap operas, talk shows, and popular music, all of which are broadcast on the national radio stations. There are some stations with broadcasts in Mayan languages that focus on Maya issues.

SERVICES

Telephone

Avid phone users, Guatemala had over 22 million mobile phoneline subscribers in 2024, larger than the population as a whole, though this is partly due to many having one phone for work and another for private calls. The two main companies offering phone and data packages are the market leader Tigo and Claro, which is owned by the Mexican telecom giant América Móvil.

Visitors to Guatemala arriving with an unlocked phone can easily find a Claro or Tigo SIM card with a daily or weekly package, and only need ID like a passport to purchase one.

Almost every Guatemalan has a cell phone even if they don't have a landline at home. The country code for Guatemala is +502, and it's now necessary to use an additional digit at the beginning of the typical seven-digit phone number: 2 for Guatemala City numbers; 5 for cell phone numbers; 6 for the suburbs of Guatemala City; and 7 for outside Guatemala City. To dial abroad from Guatemala, dial 00 followed by the country code.

Most people answer the phone in Guatemala by saying "*Bueno*" or "*Alo*" and waiting for your response.

USEFUL TELEPHONE NUMBERS

Country Code +502

A twenty-four-hour emergency service called ASISTUR, operated by INGUAT, the Guatemalan Tourism Agency, offers assistance for all types of emergencies (accidents, assaults, theft, legal issues) on the numbers 1500 or 2290-2810 (www.asistur.gt/en)

Police 110, 120, 137, 138

Ambulance 110, 120 123, 125, 128

Fire 110, 122, 123

INTERNET AND SOCIAL MEDIA

Guatemala has the largest internet market in Central America with over 11 million users in 2024, which represents about 65 percent of the population. Broadband adoption has been low due to the costs, so most users rely on mobile access via their phones and tablets.

The increasing availability of Wi-Fi in hotels, restaurants, and cafés in cities and tourist areas has seen a rapid decline in the fortunes of the once ubiquitous old-school internet cafés. However, if you'd rather tap out emails on an antiquated PC with some of the letters rubbed off the keyboard, or need to print something out, you can still find the odd internet café here and there, usually filled with kids doing schoolwork, playing video games, or chatting with friends.

Social media is hugely popular in Guatemala, with almost as many registered Facebook members as there are internet users. WhatsApp is the most popular messaging app and is used by Guatemalans of all generations. You will get a faster response by messaging a hotel, restaurant, or any other small business on WhatsApp than by emailing them.

Facebook is the most popular social media app, followed by TikTok, Instagram, X, and Telegram. The rise of TikTok has been driven by younger users, while older users prefer to stick with Facebook and video sharing sites like YouTube.

CONCLUSION

Guatemala is a welcoming country that never fails to impress. Caribbean and Pacific shores bookend a dramatic highland landscape of volcanoes and crater lakes forged from furious eruptions and tectonic quakes, and vast swaths of dense rainforest that shelter a dizzying diversity of natural and national treasures, among them the majestic ruins of ancient Maya pyramids and palaces.

Forged from a tumultuous history and scarred by a decades-long civil war, Guatemala is also a land that is divided by history into Westernized Ladinos and modern Maya, who make up the majority of the country's indigenous population. The people of Guatemala are as difficult to sum up as the country's physical geography.

Life for many is lived both in the past and the present; some are disenfranchised, but all continue to strive for a better future for their families. The challenges are not few: there are limited opportunities for the poor, a history of corrupt and inefficient governments, and a traditionalist view of gender roles that impacts Guatemala's women and girls the hardest.

Thankfully, the years of violence and terror that scarred the country and its people during the civil war are over. While the country is still coming to terms with that past, it has also moved on and today celebrates its unique combination of indigenous culture, Spanish heritage, and modern Western influence in a way that it could not before.

Among what makes Guatemala such an interesting place to live in or visit is the diversity of the cultures that you'll encounter, from Ladino and Maya to Garifuna and Afro-Guatemalan. Despite their differences, it is the warm and welcoming people of Guatemala, whatever their background, that will leave a lasting impression.

The glue that holds Guatemalan society together is family, a core belief in blood ties that shapes the way people live, love, and interact. As a visitor, it will naturally take time to build true friendships and earn a place at the family table, but from day one you will feel the warmth of a people who still strike up conversations with the people sitting next to them on a chicken bus, or a bench in the plaza. There is also a wild side to Guatemala—it is a land of firecracker fiestas, unpredictable schedules; music-blasting, colorful chicken buses; and bustling markets, but that's also partly what makes it so engaging. Come with an open mind and an open heart and this country will enchant you.

FURTHER READING

Asturias, Miguel Ángel. *Men of Maize*. Penguin Classics, 2024.

Asturias, Miguel Ángel. *Mr. President*. Penguin Classics, 2022.

Benz, Stephen Connely. *Guatemalan Journey*. Austin: University of Texas Press, 2010.

Carlsen, Williams. *Jungle of Stone: The Extraordinary Journey of John L. Stephens and Frederick Catherwood, and the Discovery of the Lost Civilization of the Maya*. Mariner Books, 2017.

Cervantes, Fernando. *Conquistadores*. Penguin Books, 2021.

Chapman, Peter. *Bananas: How the United Fruit Company Shaped the World*. Edinburgh: Canongate Books, 2009.

Coe, Michael D. and Houston, Stephen. *The Maya*. Thames and Hudson, 2015.

Drew, David. *The Lost Chronicles Of The Maya Kings*. London: Weidenfeld & Nicolson, 2006.

Goldman, Francisco. *The Art of Political Murder: Who Killed Bishop Gerardi?* London: Atlantic Books, 2010.

Grandin, Greg; Levenson, Deborah T.; and Oglesby, Elizabeth. *The Guatemala Reader: History, Culture, Politics*. Durham, NC: Duke University Press, 2011.

Halfon, Eduardo. *Canción*. Bellevue Literary Press, 2022.

Martin, Simon and Grube, Nikolai. *Chronicle of the Maya Kings and Queens*. Thames and Hudson, 2008.

Menchú, Rigoberta. *I, Rigoberta Menchú: An Indian Woman in Guatemala*. New York: Verso, 2010.

Page, Lachlan. *The Smuggler's Apprentice of Guatemala*. WJ Press, 2023.

Schlesinger, Stephen and Kinzer, Stephen. *Bitter Fruit: The Story of the American Coup in Guatemala*. Boston: Harvard University Press, 2005.

Tedlock, Dennis. *Popol Vuh*. New York: Touchstone, 1996.
Vargas Llosa, Mario. *Harsh Times*. London: Faber & Faber, 2022.

Wilkinson, Daniel. *Silence on the Mountain: Stories of Terror Betrayal and Forgetting in Guatemala*. Duke University Press, 2006.

Wright, Ronald. *Time Among the Maya: Travels in Belize, Guatemala and Mexico*. London: Eland Publishing, 2020.

USEFUL APPS

Travel and Transportation

Uber The popular ride-sharing app covers the major cities, though drivers are restricted from pick-ups and drop-offs at some airports. Where the app does work, it can help to cut journey costs considerably. **InDrive** and **Cabify** are two alternative ride-hailing apps popular locally. In Guatemala City, electric moped scooters are available via **Yego**.

If you want to drive in Guatemala, **Waze** has the most up-to-date info on routes, journey times, and alternatives if roads are blocked or traffic jammed. Other useful navigate apps include **Maps.me** and, of course, **Google Maps**.

Plan journeys on public transport using **Moovit**. In Guatemala City, navigate the bus rapid transit system using the dedicate **Transmetro** app. Riders will need to buy a Tarjeta Ciudadano travel card ahead of time as cash is not accepted on board.

Food and Shopping

If you're hungry but don't fancy going out, you can order food for delivery via **Hugo** and **PedidosYa**. Cities currently serviced include Guatemala City and Antigua, and both apps can also be used to order groceries and medicines. **Uber Eats** offers an alternative food delivery service while its sister app **Cornershop** offers supermarket and grocery deliveries.

When it comes to shopping online **Mercado Libre** offers a reliable service locally. **Amazon** does ship to Guatemala, but delivery times may vary and shipping fees can be high. **Facebook Marketplace** offers a popular local alternative.

Communication and Socializing

The most handy app for communication in Guatemala—and that includes businesses as well as people—is **WhatsApp**. For socializing as well as finding events locally to you, **Facebook** is the local choice. **Eventos**, **MeetUp**, **TimeOut** all also offer options for meeting people in Guatemala.

Speaking even just a bit of Spanish will open doors for you. Brush up on your language skills using **DuoLingo**, **Babel**, and **Bussu**. Whether you're struggling to make sense of a menu, a road sign, or your taxi driver, you can rely on **Google Translate** with its own voice, image, and text features. It also has an offline feature for when you are off the beaten path and connectivity might be limited.

PICTURE CREDITS

INDEX

Acknowledgment

I would like to dedicate this book to my beloved father, Derek Maddicks, who left us too soon in the midst of the Covid-19 epidemic and who lives on in the hearts of all who knew him. Thanks also to Francisco Maddicks, my son and travel buddy who inspires me to spread the word about the wonders of Latin America that we encounter on our research trips through the region.